About Island Press

Since 1984, the nonprofit organization Island Press has been stimulating, shaping, and communicating ideas that are essential for solving environmental problems worldwide. With more than 1,000 titles in print and some 30 new releases each year, we are the nation's leading publisher on environmental issues. We identify innovative thinkers and emerging trends in the environmental field. We work with world-renowned experts and authors to develop cross-disciplinary solutions to environmental challenges.

Island Press designs and executes educational campaigns in conjunction with our authors to communicate their critical messages in print, in person, and online using the latest technologies, innovative programs, and the media. Our goal is to reach targeted audiences—scientists, policymakers, environmental advocates, urban planners, the media, and concerned citizens—with information that can be used to create the framework for long-term ecological health and human well-being.

Island Press gratefully acknowledges major support of our work by The Agua Fund, The Andrew W. Mellon Foundation, The Bobolink Foundation, The Curtis and Edith Munson Foundation, Forrest C. and Frances H. Lattner Foundation, The JPB Foundation, The Kresge Foundation, The Oram Foundation, Inc., The Overbrook Foundation, The S.D. Bechtel, Jr. Foundation, The Summit Charitable Foundation, Inc., and many other generous supporters.

The opinions expressed in this book are those of the author(s) and do not necessarily reflect the views of our supporters.

TACTICAL
URBANISM

TACTICAL URBANISM

Short-term Action for Long-term Change

Mike Lydon and Anthony Garcia

Washington | Covelo | London

Island Press is a trademark of The Center for Resource Economics.

Book and cover design by Katie King Rumford (katiekingrumford.com)

Library of Congress Control Number: 2014948288

Photo on page iii: *Chair Bombs* by Aurash Khawarzad

Printed on recycled, acid-free paper

Manufactured in the United States of America
10 9 8 7 6 5 4 3 2 1

Keywords: Bouquinistes, Build a Better Block, Ciclovía, design thinking, DIY urbanism, food trucks, guerilla urbanism, guerilla wayfinding, intersection repair, mobile services, New Urbanism, Park(ing) Day, open streets, parklet, Pavement to Plazas, play streets, radical connectivity, temporary intervention, traffic calming, urban hacking, Walk [Your City]

TO OUR GRANDFATHERS,

—

William Dunham and Carlos Tepedino

CONTENTS

—

FOREWORD

—

ANDRÉS DUANY

As the dismal prospects of the twenty-first century gradually become clear, it also becomes clear that some of the most promising ideas about cities are coalescing as Tactical Urbanism. The book that proves this is in your hands; it remains only to contextualize my claim.

Two wholly new urbanisms have emerged to engage the circumstances of the twenty-first century: Tactical and XL (or Extra Large). This pairing shows that Rem Koolhaas's prescient formulation of S, M, L, and XL projects is incomplete. It is missing the XS: the Extra Small category represented by Tactical Urbanism.

The architectural world is currently fascinated by the Extra Large (in fact, the March 2014 *Architectural Record*, arriving the very week I am writing this, is dedicated to the XL category). The XL are projects such as regional shopping malls, so immense and complex that they subsume urbanism. They are presumed to intensify urban life. They certainly provide an unprecedented opportunity for iconic architecture, and also the opportunity for the most spectacular failures.

But even the iconic successes of XL have bleak prospects. Most of the projects are cynical panderings to the insecurities of Asian and Middle Eastern nouveaux riches. As James Kunstler argues, they have no future socially, ecologically, economically, or politically. The XLs are indeed magnificent, but they are like dinosaurs: Each is individually dependent on the acquisition of tons of fodder, while the mammals survive by foraging for ounces. Like the mammals, the XS Tactical interventions can collectively achieve the urban biomass of an XL project.

The glamorous XLs are high-tech monocultures subject to the requirements for cheap energy, assumed collective behaviors, and top-down protocols—all unsustainable. I sometimes think the CIA has recovered its vaunted cleverness to destroy America's competitors in Asia by embedding our megalomaniac XL designs in their cities and equipping their kids in our architecture schools with economically unsustainable and socially catastrophic urban design concepts.

As these beasts stumble and wither, there will be greater worldwide interest in Tactical Urbanism: decentralized, bottom-up, extraordinarily agile, networked, low-cost, and low-tech. It will be the urban planning equivalent of the iPhone replacing the mainframe.

Why did Tactical Urbanism emerge just now? Because the United States has already experienced those awful ideas that are now being exported. Our consultants do not build XL projects here, because we have learned not to trust them. Our society has created the antibodies that prevent them: the pervasive NIMBYs and intractable bureaucracies conceived to make such projects difficult, if not impossible. However, so badly has our society been damaged by these failures that now, even small projects become impossible.

The brilliance of Tactical Urbanism is not just that it is an agile response to the reduced circumstances of the twenty-first century but that it has turned the opposition, private and public, into a motive. The frustrated and frustrating process of public participation begins skeptically and tentatively and then picks up as confidence is reestablished with Tactical Urbanist demonstrations.

Tactical Urbanism is pure American know-how. It is the common sense that housed, fed, and prospered an entire continent of penniless immigrants. We need to think this way again—and, may I add, with admiration that both XL and XS require a scurrilous sense of fun. Without that, you just won't *get* Tactical Urbanism. What a great filter for admission to some very good company.

PREFACE

—

A crisis is a terrible thing to waste.

—PAUL ROMER

We started our firm, The Street Plans Collaborative, in the middle of the worst economy either of us—and our parents—had ever known. As a result, we treated our nascent company with frugal conservatism but one that was generous with our respective communities, with our time. So it's no wonder that we discovered the Tactical Urbanism ethos in the work of those around us, because we were using its core philosophy to incrementally grow our business.

Our ambition was, and remains, to combine planning and design consulting with what our firm now calls research-advocacy projects. To this last point, when we started our careers there was no YouTube, blogs and Facebook were just becoming a thing, and no one had heard of Twitter. Well, that's all changed, and quickly. We've never been so connected online yet so far away in our communities. But our current technology and the ethos of overlapping open source movements have played a pivotal role in our ability to learn from others and in the dissemination of Tactical Urbanism. We'll explore this key point further in chapter 3, but we want to make clear that although this book comes with a price tag, much of the information contained herein does not. And for that we're grateful.

When you have finished reading this book, we hope you feel empowered. We're writing this book because so many others have inspired and empowered us, as you will read in the discovery stories that follow. We are now more excited than ever by the endless number of creative projects that are emerging daily, and we believe strongly that Tactical Urbanism enables people to not only envision change but to help create it. This is powerful stuff. Thanks for reading.

Mike's Story

Letter writing is the only device for combining solitude with good company.

—LORD BYRON

With a planning degree fresh in hand, I left graduate school in Ann Arbor, Michigan for Miami, Florida in 2007 to return to Duany Plater-Zyberk and Company, where I had interned. I had worked primarily on Miami 21, an effort that entailed replacing the city's convoluted and archaic zoning code with one that streamlined the development process and aimed for results more in line with twenty-first-century planning ideals: transit-oriented development, green buildings, and more sensitive transitions between existing single-family neighborhoods and fast-changing commercial corridors. The project—the largest application of a form-based code at the time and maybe still—was innovative and complex, a dream assignment for a young and idealistic planner like me.

Yet in the first few months I began discovering the limitation of the planner's toolbox, especially in conveying the technical aspect of the Miami 21 effort to the public. I was still passionate about making a change and looked for additional opportunities to influence my newly adopted city.

My lonely 8-mile bicycle commute from Miami Beach to Miami's Little Havana neighborhood seemed like a good place to start. At work I voiced concerns to my colleagues that more could be done to make Miami a safe, inviting place for cyclists, and I was dedicating my free time to local bicycle advocacy. My boss at the time, Elizabeth Plater-Zyberk, heard me discussing this at the office and advised that I send an op-ed to the *Miami Herald* explaining why—and how—the city should improve conditions for bicyclists. "Make Miami a Bicycle-Friendly City" was the title of my December 2007 op-ed in the *Miami Herald*. In it I claimed that Miami was choosing not to compete with other leading American cities in attracting and retaining talent, ensuring low-cost transportation options, and, ultimately, fulfilling the long-term promises of Miami 21.

Among other ideas, I suggested that the city hire a bicycle coordinator, undertake a comprehensive bicycle master plan, and shift policy to "complete its streets." I also suggested that Miami could adapt Bogotá, Colombia's Ciclovía, a weekly livability initiative that transforms approximately 70 miles (112 km) of interconnected streets into linear parks that are free of motor vehicles.

During this time I also started blogging on the popular Transit Miami blog, where I met Tony, and worked closely with the newly formed Green Mobility Network advocacy organization and Emerge Miami, a dedicated but loosely organized group of young professionals looking to make a positive impact.

Together our groups helped form the city's first Bicycle Action Committee and created an action plan that could be adopted and implemented. To our amazement, our ideas for making Miami easier to navigate on bicycle were supported by Mayor Manny Diaz and his staff, who vowed to make Miami a much more bicycle-friendly city. Highlights of the plan included obtaining a League of American Bicyclists Bicycle-Friendly Community rating by 2012, priority infrastructure projects in line with upcoming capital budget expenditures, and the implementation of Bike Miami Days, the city's first Ciclovía-like event. Whereas the first two took several years of policy and physical planning advances (the city received its bronze designation in 2012), the Ciclovía-like event—or what is now popularly referred to in North America as "open streets"—rose to the top of the priority list because it was quick and relatively inexpensive. Plus, could there be a more visible initiative than closing off downtown Miami streets for social and physical activity?

To our delight, thousands of people showed up to the first event in November 2008, and not just the spandex-clad MAMILs (Middle-Aged Men in Lycra) but entire families, women of all ages, and a lot of young adults. People were not just bicycling but also walking, jogging, skating, and dancing along normally car-choked streets. The novelty of the event created an almost palpable, intoxicating energy on the street, and the impact was immediate and very visible. Furthermore, the thousands of smiling faces, banner sales for some business owners, and the noticeable absence of "car-mageddon" put a lot of people at ease, including the mayor, who gave the welcoming address before leading a ceremonial bike ride along Flagler Street.

As an event, Bike Miami Days was a success. And it served a much greater purpose: It allowed a few thousand participants to experience their city in

Bike Miami Days debuted in 2008. (Mike Lydon)

an entirely new and exciting way. It also gave them a chance to imagine a different urban future, one where walking, bicycling, and the provision of more public space could be made easier. We certainly didn't call it Tactical Urbanism at the time, but that's exactly what it was. I was hooked.

The event made me realize that I was frustrated not just with the lack of bicycle planning in Miami but with the field of urban planning. Indeed, after 18 months of working as a consultant, I had not seen any of my work result in meaningful, on-the-ground change. Perhaps I'm impatient—some say that's also a generational trait—but many planning exercises quickly revealed themselves to be just that: expensive ways to discuss the possible, with implementation perpetually on hold until a time when the politics and dollars *might* align.

Like most urban planners, I went into the profession to make a positive and visible difference in the world. To me, the goal was always to do so in the near term, not "maybe later." And although it was just a temporary event, Bike Miami Days seemed more powerful than any public workshop, charrette, or meeting I had attended. I remember thinking then, as I still believe today, that transformative infrastructure and planning projects have their place; new rail lines, bridges, or the rezoning of an entire city are difficult but certainly necessary and important projects. However, you rarely get the buy-in needed through the conventional planning process alone. To be sure, a city can't respond to its challenges merely through the exercise of planning for the long term; it must also move quickly on many, many smaller projects. Indeed, these are the ones that engage citizenry and often make the big-ticket items possible in the long run. Cities need big plans but also small tactics.

With this in mind, I began to see open streets initiatives as a possible planning tool, another way cities could reach and inspire their citizens, and a way for citizens to in turn inspire their government to embrace change. Bike Miami Days proved to be a critical tactic for building public awareness and interest in the city's incipient bicycling strategy. In many ways, it demonstrated that there, hidden in plain sight, was a diverse constituency of people searching for more opportunities to be physically active in public space. As temporary as it was, the streets became the manifestation of what planners would be lucky to create in years, not weeks.

A few months after the launch of Bike Miami Days, I was asked, alongside Collin Worth, the city's newly hired bicycle coordinator, to carry out Miami's first bicycle master plan. I really enjoyed my current job, but I embraced the opportunity. I set up a home office, had a website built by a friend of a friend for a few hundred dollars, and began doing business as a sole proprietor under the name The Street Plans Collaborative.

After completing that plan, I moved to Brooklyn, New York. I had grown increasingly enamored with the inventive work being undertaken by the New York City Department of Transportation, led by Janette Sadik-Khan: hundreds of miles of new bike lanes, several newly minted "pilot" pedestrian plazas, and Summer Streets, the city's version of Bike Miami Days. Inspired, I began to look around for other activists and communities advancing what I saw as a healthy balance of planning *and* doing, leaders who looked to instigate change. Tony and I had worked together for several years on Transit Miami, so we decided to become partners, and in 2010 we officially incorporated Street Plans as a company.

As the year progressed, I continued researching not only open streets programs but a variety of short-term, often creative projects that were having a big impact on city policy and city streets. That fall I traveled to New Orleans for a retreat with a group of friends and colleagues who sometimes identify as "NextGen," a spinoff of the Congress for the New Urbanism. I shared notes on a groundswell of seemingly unrelated low-cost urban interventions occurring across mid-recession America.

With the purpose of giving more shape—and a recognizable name—to the ideas I shared in New Orleans, we assembled *Tactical Urbanism: Short-Term Action, Long-Term Change*, Volume 1, in 2011 and provided the free digital document on SCRIBD. I posted the link on our company's research web page and then sent the link to my colleagues and left for a needed vacation. I would have been happy if five or six of the twenty or so New Orleans retreat attendees read the twenty-five-page booklet.

In less than 2 months the document was viewed or downloaded more than 10,000 times. Although I was confident Tactical Urbanism was a potentially powerful and discernible trend, the interest exceeded all our expectations.

By the fall of 2011 our company had moved from just documenting Tactical Urbanism to integrating it into our professional practice. My friend and colleague Aurash Khawarzad suggested that we gather people together to share information, ideas, and best practices. It was then that we decided to test the interest in Tactical Urbanism beyond the digital realm. Soon thereafter, the Queens-based arts collective Flux Factory lent us their event space in a converted Long Island City greeting card factory, and we partnered with numerous organizations to produce the first Tactical Urbanism Salon. For nearly 10 hours, 150-plus people from around North America discussed their projects, listened to others, debated, and drank free beer. Further inspired by the interest and blossoming work of so many urbanists, we decided to write and release Volume 2. We doubled the number of case studies, included a brief overview of Tactical Urbanism's history, and provided a spectrum of unsanctioned to sanctioned tactics; many of the latter moved to the former as we wrote.

Since the Queens event, we've co-produced five more salons in Philadelphia, Santiago, Memphis, Louisville, and Boston. And at the time of this writing, the full series of publications have been viewed or downloaded more than 275,000 times by people in more than one hundred countries. This includes the Spanish and Portuguese version of Volume 2; Volume 3, which focuses on Central and South America, co-authored with Ciudad Emergente, a Santiago, Chile–based social enterprise focused on enriching public space;

Mike Lydon spray paints a "sharrow" during a Build a Better Block initiative in Middlesboro, Kentucky. (Isaac Kremer for Discover Downtown Middlesboro)

and Volume 4, researched and written by our partners at Melbourne-based CoDesign Studio, which focuses on examples in Australia and New Zealand. We continue to lead workshops around the world, working with students, professionals, and citizens to teach them how they might use Tactical Urbanism to create a more collaborative approach to city and placemaking.

To my surprise, the simple act of writing an op-ed has led to many great people, opportunities, ideas, and challenges. It also provides proof that big things can happen when you start small.

Tony's Story

It was during a Memorial Day weekend trip to New York with my then 4-year-old son that I first started thinking about Tactical Urbanism. We had planned a special father–son trip to the city, and one of our stops was a mega toy store in Times Square. Directly in front of this location was where Broadway had been converted into a pedestrian plaza with lawn chairs and orange plastic barrels the very morning we were there. It was a startling change.

After making our purchase and leaving the toy store, my son and I settled in the newly formed plaza. As someone who had lived in New York for several years and had been visiting since childhood, I never really sat in Times Square and *enjoyed* it. Not until that day. The conversion was so new that people were still crowding the sidewalk and unsure about how to interact with the space. We were some of the first that morning who confidently stepped off the sidewalk and sat down. Others followed suit, but it was slow. We lingered there for a while, playing with his new toy and simply enjoying the city—something that you couldn't really do before.

The immediacy of it struck a chord in me, not only because of my advocacy experience in Miami with megaprojects such as Miami 21 and the half-cent transit tax, but also because of my professional work and the feeling that it was near impossible to get anything done. Here was a street retrofitted into a public space that didn't take millions of dollars and a decade to complete. It *felt* quick and easy and was totally effective.

This approach to planning resonated with me. I had been trying to live in an urban context in Miami since my return from college at NYU, and I found the experience lacking. I realized that many of the things I had come to love about living in a city were gone, namely great transit and abundant public space options. Returning to the suburban campus of the University of Miami, I went through a major period of urbanism withdrawal and sought to educate myself about the city I loved and try to make it into more of the city I expected.

I started to attend public meetings, city commission meetings, and planning board meetings and to write letters to the editor and go to any event that had to do with infrastructure or the functioning of the city. I immersed myself in the civic life of the city. I yearned for a better way to interact with my city government and make a substantial contribution to the development of the city, yet I found few options other than being a municipal employee or hired consultant.

As a way of channeling this civic energy, I started writing for, and would later be the editor of, a local blog called Transit Miami that focused on transportation and urban planning in Miami. Blogs were relatively new then, another reflection of how technology was affecting the city. Through my writing I became heavily involved in the aforementioned Miami 21 approval process, the implementation of the 2002 half-cent transit tax, and the rise of bike culture in Miami. These experiences crystalized in my mind several ideas presented in this book.

The first was how dysfunctional the public planning process had become. I was excited about the prospect of my hometown having a new, forward-thinking zoning code. What I was not prepared for was how onerous the approval process would be for a code so large and complex. The project had gone through hundreds of public meetings and was significantly better than its predecessor yet was still attacked for being drafted behind closed doors. Although the resulting form-based code was ultimately approved, it was the process that had the greatest impact on me. No matter how progressive it was, a large percentage of people were against the code (to say nothing of the percentage who didn't even understand it), leading to delays and changes. Taken together with the dozens of land use attorneys, developers, and lobbyists, the approval meetings were a dizzying circus of opposition. I kept wondering, how can we ensure a sincere and thorough public process, and reform large-scale zoning systems, without having it turn into this?

Around the same time, Miami-Dade County approved a half-cent sales tax that was intended to fund a greatly expanded Metrorail network. I was proud to have voted for the item, yet several years passed and no major expansion was realized. Although there was full public support for the building of 80 new miles of transit, there was little municipal appetite for implementation of the costly system. A decade later, very little has been built, and the region needs transit more than ever. The failure of the half-cent tax offered another lesson: Megaprojects are not going to solve our problems, and we need to find a workaround to the challenge of building and retrofitting our cities to align more closely with the vision of plans such as Miami 21 if they are to be successful. I began to see small-scale changes as part of the answer to the stalled momentum of large projects.

It was in the growth of bicycle culture and infrastructure in Miami that I first witnessed how small-scale changes can lead to longer-term results. From Bike Miami Days and Critical Mass to the growth of bike infrastructure, there were a string of low-cost projects that individually were not so important but together convinced me that small, often short-term, easy-to-implement projects could have just as powerful an impact on the culture of a city as the megaprojects.

After grad school I worked at Chael Cooper & Associates Architecture, taking on both large-scale mixed-use development projects and small-scale residential projects. The same focus on large projects that I witnessed in my advocacy work was also present in my professional work; some of the projects we worked on promised to transform neighborhoods. Yet it turned out to be the smaller projects that were the most rewarding because they were tangible and measurable in a very short time, whereas little at the larger scale was actually built.

It was at this time that I took my son to New York and experienced what we would later call Tactical Urbanism firsthand. After that trip I traveled for a urban design charrette and became aware of the ways that inexpensive, short-term solutions were being implemented (because of either government inaction, the economy, or a lack of consensus). Back at home, fewer building projects came into the office, and I found myself more excited about civic involvement and street design than buildings.

After a time I had a flourishing start-up that resulted from my volunteer work in the community, and I became closer friends with Mike Lydon, having worked with him on Transit Miami for several years. We had a shared passion for remaking our cities, and we both knew that the key to that transformation was the street. Soon after we embarked on our solo careers, we decided to become partners and formally incorporated Street Plans.

Hundreds of projects, salons, workshops, and lectures later, we continue to evolve and refine our thinking on city making in the twenty-first century. And although we know that tactical projects alone are not a panacea for our cities, the underlying low-cost and iterative approach can be applied in a variety of ways to address the challenges of the coming decades. Of course, we know that every city is not New York or Miami, and what we've learned from the many projects we've worked on together is that the challenges affecting our cities are just as numerous in the dense urban core as they are in our metropolitan suburbs. The challenge for urbanists everywhere will be how to find low-cost, iterative responses for each.

ACKNOWLEDGMENTS

—

Although it would be impossible to thank everyone involved in supporting this book, we'd first like to thank our families for putting up with us during the writing and editing process. A big thanks goes to the many people who have shared their projects, critiques, and writings, either directly or in our incredibly rich ecosystem of digital media outlets. In particular, we thank Elisa Colombani, Kristin Villasuso, Russell Preston, Isaac Kremer, Howard Blackson, Richard Oram, Andrés Duany, Doug Kelbaugh, David Vega-Barachowitz, Aaron Naparstek, Ronald Woudstra, Shin-pei Tsay, Aurash Khawarzad, Jason Roberts, Andrew Howard, Daniel Lerch, Matt Tomasulo, David Jurca, Nate Hommel, Mark Lakeman, Greg Raisman, Doug Farr, Charles Marohn, Eliza Harris, Ian Rasmussen, Karja Hansen, Matt Lambert, Edward Erfurt, Faith Cable Kumon, Jim Kumon, Patrick Piuma, Randy Wade, Ellen Dunham-Jones, Ellen Gottschling, Erin Barnes, Tommy Pacello, Dan Bartman, Luisa Oliveira, Pat Brown, Sarah Newstok, Jaime Ortiz, Kay Cheng, Jennifer Krouse, Bonnie Ora Sherk, Brent Toderian, Kylie Legge, Julie Flynn, Kara Wilbur, Chiara Camponeschi, Javier Vergara Petrescu, Mariko Davidson, Blaine Merker, Jake Levitas, Graham McNally, Philip Toms, Victor Dover, Jason King, Jose Carlos Mota, and Jaime Correa.

A billboard converted into swings by architect Didier Faustino for the Shenzhen–Hong Kong Bi-City Biennial of Urbanism and Architecture provides whimsy but also highlights the possibility of repurposing this ubiquitous type of urban infrastructure. (Faustino, Didier [b. 1968] © Copyright. *Double Happiness*. Photograph of the Installation at the Shenzhen–Hong Kong Bi-City Biennial of Urbanism and Architecture, 2009) Digital Image © The Museum of Modern Art/Licensed by SCALA / Art Resource, NY

01 DISTURBING THE ORDER OF THINGS

—

The lack of resources is no longer an excuse not to act. The idea that action should only be taken after all of the answers and the resources have been found is a sure recipe for paralysis. The planning of a city is a process that allows for corrections; it is supremely arrogant to believe that planning can be done only after every variable has been controlled.

—JAIME LERNER
Architect, former mayor of Curitiba, Brazil

If you visited Times Square on the Friday before Memorial Day in 2009, you, along with approximately 350,000 others, would have found a hostile urban environment. Walking into the district, you'd find the famed public space dominated by trucks spewing noxious fumes, impatient taxis blaring horns, and cars turning across your feet despite a pedestrian signal in your favor. You'd lament the false advertising: Times Square is not a square at all but a traffic-clogged bowtie wound tightly around midtown Manhattan's bulging neck. It's likely you never would have found a momentary reprieve from the chaos to observe what draws so many tourists there in the first place: the energy, the bright lights of Broadway, the spectacle of it all.

Yet if you returned *after* the same Memorial Day weekend, you would have experienced a very different place. The sidewalks, still full of life, would be noticeably less congested. The noise from the street would no longer seem as deafening. And to your astonishment, you would discover hundreds of people smiling, chatting, and taking photographs while they sat in foldable lawn chairs placed in the middle of the street. With space to look up and around to admire the lights you would realize that the new and somewhat

LEFT: Traffic-choked Times Square before pedestrianization left little room for people. (Courtesy of New York Department of Transportation)

RIGHT: Using temporary materials, a Times Square opened to people brought economic, social, and safety benefits, including for those driving. (Courtesy of New York Department of Transportation)

makeshift public space is where, just days before, cars and trucks battered all senses. Even if you didn't know the term, you would have just discovered the power and potential of Tactical Urbanism.

What Is Tactical Urbanism?

Merriam-Webster's defines *tactical* as "of or relating to small-scale actions serving a larger purpose" or "adroit in planning or maneuvering to accomplish a purpose." Translated to cities, Tactical Urbanism is an approach to neighborhood building and activation using short-term, low-cost, and scalable interventions and policies. Tactical Urbanism is used by a range of actors, including governments, business and nonprofits, citizen groups, and individuals. It makes use of open and iterative development processes, the efficient use of resources, and the creative potential unleashed by social interaction. It is what Professor Nabeel Hamdi calls making plans without the usual preponderance of planning.[1] In many ways, Tactical Urbanism is a learned response to the slow and siloed conventional city building process. For citizens, it allows the immediate reclamation, redesign, or reprogramming of public space. For developers or entrepreneurs, it provides a means of collecting design intelligence from the market they intend to serve. For advocacy organizations, it is a way to show what is possible to garner public and political support. And for government, it's a way to put best practices into, well, practice—and quickly!

tac·ti·cal   \ˈtak-ti-kəl \
adjective

(1): of or relating to small-scale actions serving a larger purpose (2): adroit in planning or maneuvering to accomplish a purpose

Because the places people inhabit are never static, Tactical Urbanism doesn't propose one-size-fits-all *solutions* but intentional and flexible *responses*. The former remains the fixation of numerous and overlapping disciplines in the urban development fields, which assume that most variables affecting cities can be controlled now and into the distant future. The latter rejects this notion and embraces the dynamism of cities. This reframing invites a new conversation about local resiliency and helps cities *and* citizens together explore a more nuanced and nimble approach to citymaking, one that can envision long-term transformation but also adjust as conditions inevitably change. How this is done effectively is a focus of this book.

Of course we recognize that not all city-building efforts lend themselves to the tactical approaches we outline in this book; we don't advocate using temporary materials to pilot-test bridges or prototype skyscrapers. When done well, large-scale projects can be catalytic, if not iconic. The value of Tactical Urbanism is in breaking through the gridlock of what we call the Big Planning

Cheap lawn chairs and orange traffic barrels were used to test the temporary closure of Times Square to automobiles. (Photo by Nina Munteanu, first appeared on
ToulouseLeTrek.com)

process (a nod to author Nicco Mele's *End of Big* thesis, which we'll explore further in chapter 3) with incremental projects and policies that can be adjusted
on the fly while never losing sight of long-term and large-scale goals.

Tactical Urbanism can be used to initiate new places or help repair existing
ones. For example, when Boston's $22 billion "Big Dig" buried the Central
Artery expressway and made room for the 15-acre Rose Kennedy Greenway,
the new public green space needed to be activated.[2] In a 2010 editorial, the
Boston Globe asserted, "What could be a monument to Boston's collective
spirit is instead a victim of the region's parochial rhythms."[3] Architecture
critic Robert Campbell put it this way: "There are things to look at but nothing to do."[4] In response to his critique, and many others, the Rose Kennedy
Greenway Conservancy began activating the forlorn spaces; demonstration
gardens, street art, food trucks, and low-cost movable tables and chairs have
breathed new life into the greenway. These low-cost modifications were
never part of the master plan per se but demonstrate that improving otherwise lifeless public spaces need not cost millions of dollars.

Tactical Urbanism is not alone in its use of lower-cost, iterative development processes. The manufacturing industry, for example, often holds up the famed Toyota Way, which uses a continuous improvement process to achieve long-term goals.[5] Similarly, tech entrepreneurs look to the tenets of The Lean Start-Up, which is a product development method advocating rapid prototyping as the inception of the deliberately agile "Build–Measure–Learn" product development cycle. The idea is that each revolution quickly improves on the last until a product is ready for the market, if only in beta form.[6] These concepts have gained currency in other professional disciplines including urban planning. We'll explore how these ideas relate to the development of neighborhoods in chapters 2 and 5.

Through our research and work, we have identified a burgeoning catalogue of Tactical Urbanism projects that respond to outdated policies and planning processes with innovative transportation, open space, and

Lightweight interventions and bold public art brought new life and attention to Boston's underwhelming Rose Kennedy Greenway. (Mike Lydon)

small-scale building initiatives. These projects often result from the direct participation of citizens in the creation and activation of their neighborhood, or the creative work of formal entities, such as nonprofits, developers, and government. Collectively, they demonstrate time and again that short-term action can create long-term change.

Tactical Urbanism is frequently applied to what urban sociologist William "Holly" Whyte called the "huge reservoir of space yet untapped by imagination."[7] Today's reservoirs—vacant lots, empty storefronts, overly wide streets, highway underpasses, surface parking lots, and other underused public spaces—remain prominent in our towns and cities and have become the targets of entrepreneurs, artists, forward-thinking government officials, and civic-minded "hacktivists." Such groups increasingly view the city as a laboratory for testing ideas in real time, and their actions have led to a variety of creative and entrepreneurial initiatives realized in the rise of food trucks, pop-up stores, better block initiatives, chair bombing, parklets, shipping con-tainer markets, do-it-yourself (DIY) bike lanes, guerrilla gardens, and other hallmarks of the Tactical Urbanism movement. These interventions were never anticipated by a master plan but provide a needed dose of whimsy and also help users and passersby not only envision a different future but expe-rience it too. And therein lies the seductive power of Tactical Urbanism: It creates tactile proposals for change instead of plans or computer-generated renderings that remain abstract.

DIY Urbanism Versus Tactical Urbanism

Life hacking. Making. The End of Expertise. The Pinterest or Ikea effect.[8] Whatever you want to call it, the resurgence of DIY culture is a well-documented phenomenon with analogues in the built environment.[9] DIY urbanism includes pop-up urbanism, user-generated urbanism, insurgent urbanism, guerrilla urbanism, and urban hacking. DIY urbanism blends a spirit of entrepreneurial activism with public art, design, architecture, engineering, technology, and notions of progressive urbanism.

So how do all these urbanisms relate to the one that is the subject of this book? It's simple: Not all DIY urbanism efforts are tactical, and not all

RIGHT: Yarnbombing can be a beautiful DIY improvement, but it is generally not tactical. (Squid Tree by Lorna and Jill Watt, 2013, knitsforlife.com/yarn-bombs)

Tactical Urbanism initiatives are DIY. For example, the international practice of yarnbombing (the crocheting of street signs, bike racks, statues, and so on) is a colorful DIY act bringing creativity (and possibly mildew) to any streetscape, yet it is not usually intended to instigate long-term change, such as revising an outdated policy or responding to a deficiency of infrastructure. We might describe it as a type of street art or opportunistic placemaking but not Tactical Urbanism.

DIY Urbanism is the expression of the individual, or at most a small group of actors, which can also describe Tactical Urbanism. However, we cannot ignore that Tactical Urbanism may also be initiated by municipal departments, government, developers, and nonprofit organizations to test ideas or enact change without delay. Although these initiatives often begin with smaller citizen advocacy efforts, the benefits of Tactical Urbanism become clearer as they are integrated into the municipal project delivery process and capably brought to neighborhoods across the city.

Contrary to its occasional portrayal as a youthful and somewhat renegade movement, Tactical Urbanism does not consist solely of unsanctioned activity carried out under the cloak of night. Although there are compelling examples of "do tanks" (as opposed to think tanks) and "urban repair squads" brandishing cans of spray paint and repurposed shipping pallets to subvert sluggish bureaucracies, Tactical Urbanism projects exist along a spectrum of legality.[10] For example, the painting of "guerrilla crosswalks" by neighborhood residents belongs on the unsanctioned side of the spectrum and the New York City Department of Transportation's placement of lawn chairs in a car-free Times Square on the sanctioned side. No matter the instigator, the appeal of Tactical Urbanism is that people often can't tell the difference between the sanctioned and unsanctioned projects and simply appreciate the human-centered approach at the heart of this burgeoning movement.

Strategies Versus Tactics

Commonly associated with military operations, *strategies* and *tactics* are valuable terms for city building. In urban planning, strategy is developed through master planning key policy or infrastructure advancements to obtain social, environmental, and/or economic goals. Accomplishing the goal of reduced car dependency, for example, requires a strategy that may include a range of policy changes, like allowing density to increase near transit stations. The

TACTICAL
SPECTRUM

Build a Better Block
Informal Bike Parking
Intersection Repair
Guerrilla Gardening
Reclaimed Setbacks
Weed Bombing
Chair Bombing
Ad-Busting

Park(ing) Day
Park-Making
Pop-Up Town Hall
Micro-Mixing
Site Pre-Vitalization
Pop-Up Retail
Food Carts/Trucks
Mobile Vendors
Depave
Camps

Pavement to Plazas
Pavement to Parks
Open Streets
Play Streets
Pop-Up Cafes
Parkmobile

 UNSANCTIONED **TACTICS** SANCTIONED

The Tactical Urbanism spectrum: Well-considered projects that begin as unsanctioned often become sanctioned over time. (The Street Plans Collaborative)

strategy is made clear through the planning process, adopted by city leaders, and then ideally moved to implementation through achieving key objectives such as zoning changes allowing for more density.

Although this approach does work in certain contexts, entrenched interests remain recalcitrant, outdated policy barriers stymie progress, and leadership voids leave well-considered plans, and their strategies, on the shelf. This is why strategy formulation is only half the battle. Planners, developers, and advocates alike need tactics that help grease the wheels for implementation from the inside out and the outside in. In this way, our understanding of tactics departs from the observations of oft-cited urbanist and French philosopher Michel de Certeau.

In his seminal *The Practice of Everyday Life,* de Certeau argues that strategies are the formal tool of the powerful (government), and tactics serve as the

Brooklyn's ubiquitous neighborhood "street seats" are usually made from found objects and reclaimed materials. (Mike Lydon)

response of the weak (citizens). Those wielding the former are constantly in competition with those advancing the latter. The dialectic is relevant to anyone interested in observing how ordinary people alter the form or use of the built environment to serve their ever-changing needs. Sometimes referred to as bricolage, this informal process of small-scale citymaking gives neighborhoods character and is the subject of inquiry by academics interested in what's called "Everyday Urbanism."

Our view is that governments can—and should—work more tactically, just as citizens can learn to work more strategically. Strategies and tactics are therefore of equal value and should be used in concert with each other. Sure, the two are often found to be pursuing different goals, but we're more interested in how they can be used together to move our cities forward. We believe Tactical Urbanism is one tool to do so and can proactively address the tension between bottom-up and top-down processes by creating a better and more responsive environment for all. How this may be done is outlined in chapter 5.

TOP DOWN

Mayors | City Councilors | Municipal Departments

TACTICAL
URBANISM

Developers
Entrepreneurs
Business Improvement Districts

Advocacy Organizations
Artists
Planning + Design Firms

BOTTOM UP

Citizen Activists | Community Groups | Neighborhood Organizations

Tacticians are found from the bottom up, the top down, and everything in between. (The Street Plans Collaborative)

How to Reach More People and How More People Can Reach You

Whether trying to achieve more transportation options, increase access to public space, or provide a more comfortable public realm for all, the pursuit of equity is often a focus for Tactical Urbanism projects. Of course, equity is contextual and broad and can be difficult to define; what might be considered fair and equal for one group may not be considered as such for another.

Still, when it comes to providing equal opportunities for a wider range of people to participate in public decision making, many well-intentioned and functionally open urban planning processes tend to appeal to a particular demographic of people: those who are educated, maintain an interest in civic issues, and, most importantly, have spare time. Finding ways to engage the young, old, disenfranchised, and uninterested is not as easy. We've certainly struggled with it in our consulting projects.

Although public planning initiatives will never come close to obtaining 100 percent participation, well-executed Tactical Urbanism projects are one way to bring planning proposals and concepts to a wider audience (see Davis Square example later in this chapter). Rather than ask people to come to City Hall on a Tuesday evening at 6:30 p.m., proposals developed at City Hall should be brought to where people already are and tested for viability. In chapter 3, we discuss further the limitations of public involvement processes and the role Tactical Urbanism can play in widening the scope.

TACTICAL URBANISM: THREE COMMON APPLICATIONS

We have already mentioned a variety of actors who may use Tactical Urbanism and a wide range of goals that interventions may help these actors reach. The following three applications are the ones that we have found to be the most common.

- Initiated by citizens to bypass the conventional project delivery process and cut through municipal bureaucracy by protesting, prototyping, or visually demonstrating the possibility of change. This activity represents citizens exercising their "right to the city."
- As a tool for city government, developers or nonprofits to more broadly engage the public during project planning, delivery, and development processes.
- As a "phase 0" early implementation tool used by cities or developers to test projects before a long-term investment is made.

These three ways of using Tactical Urbanism are not mutually exclusive. In fact, often the first leads to the second, which leads to the third. The following section delves a bit deeper into each of these applications and provides examples.

CITIZENS DEMONSTRATING THE NEED FOR CHANGE

For citizens, Tactical Urbanism is often used as an expression of civil disobedience or simply as a way of getting things done without the burden of municipal regulation or extended timeline of public process. Targets typically include outdated policies or undesirable physical conditions. As with any form of protest, the power is derived from the use of direct action to communicate the desire and possibility for change. For example, in a park-in people temporarily narrow wide streets by parking their cars against the curb in locations where it is normally prohibited. In 2013 Buffalo's Citizens for Parkside Avenue organized the "Parkside Park-in" at rush hour to slow speeding traffic along the four-lane thoroughfare. A YouTube video captured the event and includes one advocate plainly declaring, "For years, traffic has been screaming down this street. This is not an expressway on- and off-ramp. It's a neighborhood." [11]

As walkability becomes an increasingly important metric for measuring the health of cities, "guerrilla crosswalks" have emerged as a tactic for neighborhood activists fed up with the months or years it may take to get a few white lines on the ground. Indeed, citizens from New Haven to Honolulu have taken to painting crosswalks where they don't already exist or where they are no longer visible. Although many types of interventions are implemented without controversy, the guerrilla crosswalk movement has raised municipal eyebrows in more than a few cities. For example, a February 2014 *Strong Towns* blog post titled "Don't Be Stupid, Be Flexible" admonished Honolulu officials for cracking down on minor alterations made to a zebra-striped crosswalk so that it read "Aloha." The seemingly impromptu message was intended to bring a level of humanity and awareness at an otherwise auto-dominated intersection. But the message, which was formed by simply adding a few horizontal lines to the vertical ones, was a "deviation from the standard" according to local public works officials and therefore could not be trusted. Of course, the absurdity is not lost on most: Hawaii's adherence to street design standards has led to some of the highest pedestrian fatality rates in the United States, particularly among older adults. [12]

Driven more by whimsy than protest is the now international movement of "chair bombing." This popular tactic involves transforming shipping pallets into Adirondack chairs or other forms of street furniture, which are then placed on sidewalks or in public space for anyone to enjoy. It is usually carried out by civic do-gooders looking to reverse the global urban seating deficit. The DoTank: Brooklyn group dropped several of these street seats around New York City in 2011 and touched off an international trend. [13] Pallet chairs have since become a universal symbol of the DIY and citizen-led Tactical Urbanism movement.

Although some city officials may respond negatively to unauthorized citizen activity, neighbors tend to applaud it. The resulting tension exposes the growing gap between the type of cities our regulations encourage and the

In Pittsburgh, civic-minded acts of Tactical Urbanism do not go unnoticed. (Leslie Clague for the Polish Hill Civic Association)

kind of city comforts many people want. Although there are examples of a negative government response, such as that of Honolulu, city leaders increasingly view such civic-minded activity as an opportunity to leverage citizen support into needed policy shifts and longer-term projects. We explore the transformative power of citizen-led action in the examples in chapter 4 and discuss how to decide whether an unsanctioned "guerrilla" approach is right for your project in chapter 5.

A TOOL FOR PUBLIC INVOLVEMENT

City planners and others are recognizing that Tactical Urbanism can help bridge the gap between cities and developers and citizens in the urban development process. Forward-thinking city leaders in New York City, for example, have discovered that the use of temporary pilot projects can help allay NIMBY (not in my backyard) fears as the possibilities for change are demonstrated in the short term. Other cities are catching on too. When a streetscape plan for the Davis Square neighborhood in Somerville, Massachusetts was developed in 2012 using what chief planner George Proakis criticized as a conventional top-down "design–present–defend" method, a small number of "say no to everything" neighborhood stakeholders scuttled some of the most logical public space elements in the plan. Realizing that the existing public involvement system appealed only to a few people speaking on behalf of "the public," the city switched gears and developed the Somerville by Design neighborhood planning initiative. Central to the approach is the use of Tactical Urbanism, which is being used to bring planning concepts to people physically rather than asking them to come to planning meetings to discuss proposals theoretically. The goal is to show people different opportunities in the real world so that more informed decisions may be made by a more diverse audience of people.

An early Somerville by Design initiative our firm was involved with transformed a very small public parking lot into a public "pop-up plaza" for 3 days. The plaza was envisioned in the 2012 streetscape plan rejected by the public. Popular food trucks rented some of the parking stalls, covering the project's small cost, the Public Works Department put out tables and chairs sourced from City Hall, and street performers and musicians (some planned, some not) brought an additional level of activity. The temporary transformation occurred in conjunction with a neighborhood planning charrette and effectively exposed the plaza concept to a much wider audience of people. After the 3 days were up, public meetings, comment cards put on every plaza table, and general neighborhood buzz made clear that there was much more support from the public to transform the parking lot into a public space. The city has since begun that process, proving that truly participatory planning must go beyond drawing on flip charts and maps. Moreover, the city has integrated Tactical Urbanism into other neighborhood planning processes included in the Somerville by Design initiative, both as public involvement and as project implementation stages.

PHASE 0 IMPLEMENTATION

Expectations for future successes are often at their peak as planners and the participating public conclude the formal planning process. Too often that enthusiasm and momentum wane as projects await capital budget, grant, or state and federal funding and then get caught in a web of regulatory and cumbersome project delivery processes. Tactical Urbanism can alleviate this

A small city-owned parking lot in the Davis Square neighborhood in Somerville, MA, before temporary improvements. (Dan Bartman)

condition through what we call phase 0 implementation projects. Sometimes called a placeholder project, the use of temporary materials and installations continues the momentum from the formal planning process. The project can bring immediate benefits while providing the opportunity for qualitative and quantitative data to be collected and integrated into the project design before large capital expenditures occur. (See the Times Square example in Pavement to Plazas in chapter 4.)

If the project doesn't work as planned, then the entire capital budget is not exhausted, and future designs may be calibrated to absorb the lessons learned. If done well, the small-scale and temporary changes serve as the first step in realizing lasting change. This iterative process not only creates better projects but also continues the momentum established during the conventional planning process.

One recent example of phase 0 implementation is found in the small city of Penrith, in eastern Australia. After completion of an 18-month planning process for the city's main street High Street Master Plan, Sydney-based

"Cutter Square," a 3-day pop-up plaza initiative in Somerville, MA, widened public engagement and revealed support for public space improvements. (Dan Bartman)

consultants Place Partners recommended that the City Council move forward immediately by testing out one of the plan's key recommendations: the replacement of a lightly trafficked High Street block and a vastly underused swath of asphalt with a new community park.

Knowing that the money and the political will for the project's proposed end state did not yet exist, at the suggestion of Place Partners, the City Council bravely committed $40,000 to test out a pop-up park for the period of 1 year. Our firm was invited to assist with an intensive workshop in which citizens and local stakeholders co-designed the pop-up park using a priced kit of parts preapproved by the city's public works department. The city agreed that the pop-up park would be "built" the next month.

Given the city's financial commitment and the aggressive timeline, workshop participants—business operators, architecture students, local residents, community members, and government staff—felt the work at hand was not pie-in-the-sky idea generation but real. The catch was that each of the three teams had to design their part of the project using less than $10,000 worth of materials so that the remaining $10,000 could be used for elements that would stitch the three plans into one holistic park.

As promised, the city implemented the trial park the next month. Despite mixed initial reviews, the midterm evaluation conducted by an independent consulting firm uninvolved with the initial project used data collected (traffic flow, user behavior, retail sales) over the previous 6 months and found that although some property owners remained unenthusiastic, several retailers and adjacent restaurants were happy with the project. Moreover, the public was becoming accustomed to enjoying numerous public events in the park space. In May 2014, the City Council voted to extend the pop-up park's life beyond its initial year-long commitment to March 2015[14] and have even embarked on a second pop-up park project using a similar approach.[15]

In the United States, phase 0 applications are popping up from coast to coast. Since 2007, the New York City Department of Transportation has been partnering with local business improvement districts and local advocacy groups to transform acres of asphalt into temporary plazas, curb extensions, and pedestrian refuges, some of which have already made their way to permanence (see chapter 4). In Washington, DC, the city's Office of City Planning works with property owners to establish "Temporiums" that *pre*vitalize vacant commercial space with pop-up shops and art installations.

On the West Coast, San Francisco's lauded Pavement to Parks program is dedicated to "tactical projects" such as parklets: miniature parks that replace on-street parking spaces (see chapter 4). In San Diego, developers and the Downtown Partnership are breathing life into vacant sites with a temporary "Makers Quarter" site installation called Silo, as well as adding pop-up pocket parks, mobile parklets, and urban farms to the streetscape. And Portland, Oregon, ahead of all these West Coast peers, began sanctioning citizen-led "intersection repair" projects through a municipal ordinance in 2001 (see chapter 4). Finally, Las Vegas, Albuquerque, Chicago, Salt Lake City, Providence, Atlanta, and dozens of other towns and cities from coast to coast are developing sanctioned city-led Tactical Urbanism projects and programs.

RIGHT (top): Before: An underwhelming asphalt remnant used to terminate Penrith's High Street. (Penrith City Council)

RIGHT (bottom): After: Penrith's pop-up park created a public space anchor and focal point for the city's High Street. (Penrith City Council)

The mainstreaming of Tactical Urbanism into municipal planning departments is not without its perils yet remains a promising trend because it represents a shift in how cities are looking to deliver projects.

One of the more enjoyable aspects of our ongoing consulting and research work is tracking the speed at which simple and low-cost projects move across the spectrum from the unsanctioned to the sanctioned and how they evolve from temporary projects to more permanent ones through local citizen, municipal, or private sector leadership. Yet we recognize that the promise of Tactical Urbanism will be reached only if municipal leaders and citizens alike develop a holistic, cross-disciplinary approach to bring the benefits to the places that need them most.

Why You Should Keep Reading

Tactical Urbanism is often misused as a catchall to describe everything from pub crawls to chalkboard message walls. Such activities should not be discouraged—we would never say "no" to a good bar hop—but we want this book to clarify what Tactical Urbanism is and how you can apply it effectively.

For starters, Tactical Urbanism is not an off-the-shelf solution or a list your city can check off to prove that it is responsive to new ideas. Rather, Tactical Urbanism is a method for transforming what engineer and planner Chuck Marohn calls an orderly but dumb system into one that's more chaotic but smart—one that allows emergent networks of people and their ideas to develop quality-of-life improvements at the neighborhood scale. In this way, the strength is tied directly to the process: Tactical Urbanism allows frequent corrections and demonstrates willingness and appreciation for advancing

> The inherent tension between the government and the governed is as old as cities themselves.

ideas through real-world testing. Results may vary, but the process should be trusted. Indeed, it's akin to something most of us learn by sixth grade: the scientific method.

This book is about how city leaders and citizens together can create a more responsive, efficient, and creative approach to neighborhood building.

Government clearly does a wide range of things, many of them well. However, the "silos of excellence" (as Marohn calls them) developed to administer the various government city-building services (e.g., planning, engineering, housing, public works) have created a type of discordant government software (e.g., culture, codes, policy) that eventually translates to the creation of the city's hardware (e.g., buildings, streets, parks). The core of this system has been in place for almost 100 years, and in most communities it is starting to show its age and is due for an upgrade. The task of those involved with building towns and cities today is to reintegrate the software so that a better hardware continues to emerge, one that improves the lives of residents and the experience for visitors and leads to economic success for business owners.

That being said, the inherent tension between the government and the governed is as old as cities themselves. Although the term *Tactical Urbanism* is relatively new, many of the processes, ideas, tactics, and projects we share herein are not. Chapter 2 highlights a half-dozen moments in history to demonstrate how informal, mobile, temporary, and tactical city-building initiatives have constantly altered the social, political, economic, and physical fabric of our cities.

In chapter 3, we explore how the Great Recession and the trends of returning to the city, a growing disconnect with government, and the growth of radical connectivity have supported the rise of Tactical Urbanism in the twenty-first century. If nothing stays the same, the question becomes how the lessons learned from the previous decade offer insight into how urban development will be shaped in the coming years.

We include many innovative and inspiring projects throughout the book, but chapter 4 focuses on five stories that best exemplify the power of Tactical Urbanism: Intersection Repair, Guerrilla Wayfinding, Build a Better Block, Parkmaking, and Pavement to Plazas. These tactics may be familiar to some readers, but we're willing to bet that even the most seasoned Tactical Urbanist will discover something new. Indeed, each tactic has a compelling origin story that contextualizes why the projects were developed, how they were executed, the lessons learned through implementation, and the impact they've had locally, nationally, and even internationally. Because those we profile have inspired so many great projects, four of the five stories also include an example from another time and place, demonstrating the scalability of these tactics.

Given the seemingly endless variety of social, physical, and cultural contexts for Tactical Urbanism projects, a single off-the-shelf how-to is not conceivable or advised. Moreover, the Tactical Urbanism toolkit is constantly evolving; we are continually researching and learning alongside our project partners, practitioners, and readers like you. But we do offer our best and most current advice for developing your own projects in chapter 5. We've found that successful projects have elements of a common approach that is aligned with the five principles of Design Thinking. In this case, *design* refers not to objects per se but to a specific process that should be described as "an action, a verb not a noun."[16]

The chapter begins with discussion about developing empathy and understanding for your end users. We continue by explaining how to define and select appropriate project opportunities and to decide whether your project should come in the form of a sanctioned city effort or perhaps be brought forth a little more … informally. We'll also discuss how to plan your project—yes, there has to be some planning—and explain how to move forward, including funding and finding appropriate partners. We'll also discuss how to develop prototypes, share some of our favorite materials, and walk you through the testing phase, which includes the development of metrics to help gauge your project's success and failures (yes, there will be some failures).

We complete the chapter by recommending basic due diligence for planning and implementing projects and conclude with a series of guiding questions that you might consider before embarking on your first or hundredth project.

In the Conclusion, we reflect briefly on the Tactical Urbanism movement and challenge you to use the ideas in this book to take action in your own town or city.

Before we get on with it, we want to impress on you that Tactical Urbanism has very real limitations. It's not *the* or even *one* solution for many of our most vexing urban problems. It can't solve the affordable housing crisis facing our most desirable cities, nor will it fix bridges in need of repair. It can't build high-speed rail lines, and it won't resolve the looming public sector pension crisis found in so many North American cities. If you can figure out solutions to those challenges, we'll be sure to buy your book.

But seriously, these constraints also explain Tactical Urbanism's undeniable appeal. It is a movement based on a positive vision for the future. It is about developing responses and processes that can work in large cities and small towns. It is about building social capital with your neighbors and city leaders. It is, as Nabeel Hamdi says, about "disturbing the order of things in the interest of change"[17] and creating livability gains where we all notice them most: our neighborhoods.

02

INSPIRATIONS AND ANTECEDENTS OF TACTICAL URBANISM

—

Before the city was the hamlet and the shrine and the village: before the village, the camp, the cache, the cave, the cairn; and before all these there was a disposition to social life that man plainly shares with many animal species.

—LEWIS MUMFORD
The City in History[1]

It would be nice to believe that we've discovered some entirely new form of urbanism, but the truth is that the impulse to create temporary or low-cost responses to the challenges of urban life is not new. Here, we have reframed a set of core placemaking values (temporary, low-cost, flexible, iterative, participatory) found throughout history and updated them for the digital age. From provisional Roman military encampments, to *les bouquinistes* illegally selling books along the banks of the Seine in sixteenth-century Paris, to the temporary White City of the Chicago World's Fair of 1892, the hallmarks of Tactical Urbanism have been inscribed in city-building patterns throughout history.

Today, the convergence of several social, economic, and technological trends (discussed in chapter 3) have led us and many others to rediscover the benefits of what we now call Tactical Urbanism. Ultimately, Tactical Urbanism describes the latest response to our basic human instincts: incremental and self-directed action toward increasing social capital, economic opportunity, access to food, safety from natural and human enemies, and general livability. These instincts are expressed as both macroscale strategies that facilitate lean and efficient development of buildings, streets, and parks and microscale tactics *within* the city that involve the rituals of commerce, politics, recreation, and art.

The historical precedents profiled in this chapter are not comprehensive or perfectly aligned, but they do serve as inspirations for and antecedents of Tactical Urbanism interventions. The principles are timeless. Human ingenuity aimed at improving urban life knows no profession, sector, or points along a historical timeline. We'll always have unmet needs and unexploited opportunities to enhance urban living. Those who address them directly, creatively, and efficiently will continue to guide us in the twenty-first century.

THE FIRST STREET

Streets are the backbone of a city and its largest reservoir of public space, so it is natural that we found the spirit of citizen-led urbanism in the iterative and largely horizontal process of creating what is believed to be the first urban street. The Neolithic settlement of Khoirokoitia, on the island of Cyprus, was inhabited from about 7,000 to 3,000 b.c.e., predating the use of ceramic tools by several thousand years. At its height, the village housed between 300 and 600 inhabitants.

The village consisted of round stone structures of varying sizes fronting a linear street. The buildings and the street together formed a single hilltop structure that was accessible only via a series of stairs and walkways from below; one had to walk up these access points to reach the town.[2] When completed, the street reached a length of 600 feet (185 meters). Built using rocks quarried from the Cyprian hillside, the street was built to serve the community's most basic needs: communication, mobility, trade, and security.

Its creation implies a new level of sophistication in social collaboration and construction. There was a larger plan at work for both the street and the village. Indeed, the "street" was not just the leftover space between buildings but a structure intentionally built up from the ground with controlled points of access. Without any formal, overarching government structure, Khoirokoitia's residents were the only ones responsible for the creation and maintenance of the street. They understood its importance for the survival of the village.[3]

Unlike informal paths, roads, or other ad hoc thoroughfares that almost certainly existed at the time, a common agreement was made in Khoirokoitia to ensure that the physical definition of the street would remain intact.

The first "urban" street was built in the Neolithic settlement of Khoirokoitia, on the island of Cyprus, inhabited from about 7,000 to 3,000 b.c.e. (By Ophelia2 via Wikimedia Commons)

Inhabitants were expected to respect the delineation between the public street and the private residence, which we assume that they did successfully, as evidenced by the fact that it remained intact for thousands of years. And with no other public space internal to the village, the street introduced a social function: urbanism.

Although the village residents wouldn't have considered it planning per se, the intentional organization of structures along a common artery indicates one of the first public, citizen-led planning processes in history. Because theirs was a town of hundreds (at the most), the task of bridging the gap between the needs of the people and the Council of Elders was very small. The Council of Elders simply oversaw the process not as rulers but as arbiters of consensus.[4]

Khoirokoitia's street is a demonstration of the ancient human impulse to improve and maintain the space we inhabit collectively. The truth is that both formal and informal processes have important roles to play in the creation of a city. And although it's easy to see how citizens in a village of several hundred can come together to build a single street, what happens to this vernacular spirit of citymaking when a city is home to a hundred thousand or more people? It's a question answered today in cities large and small; the creation of streets for people has become an infinitely more complex endeavor since the introduction of many transportation modes. However, the late 1960s example of the first Dutch *woonerf*, described in the next section, and the many examples found in chapter 4 give us all hope that citizens can and will continue to take back the street for its original purpose: walking, playing, selling, and socializing. Cities are for people.

THE *WOONERF*

The invention of the Dutch *woonerf* stands out because unlike many street design innovations from the last 100 years, it did not originate from the profession of traffic engineering but from citizens seeking to slow traffic in their community. Dutch for "living yard," the *woonerf* is a residential street where people who are not in cars are given priority over people who are. This is accomplished by using physical design to slow drivers down to a near walking speed so as to not crash into strategically placed trees, bollards, bike racks, and other amenities.[5]

The *woonerf* was created when a group of residents in the Dutch city of Delft grew frustrated with the growing problems related to safety, congestion, and pollution as car use increased in their compact and otherwise walkable city.[6] The municipality's lack of response inspired a group of neighbors to tear up portions of the pavement on their street in the middle of the night so that cars had to maneuver around the resulting obstruction at low speed. This citizen-led, bottom-up initiative introduced a new street type to international audiences, one that returned the street to the citizens for playing, walking, and bicycling and did not give the automobile priority.

With little evidence that the intervention disrupted daily life, the municipal government quietly ignored the citizen-led initiative and advocates pursued its formal acceptance. In 1976 the Dutch Parliament passed regulations incorporating the *woonerven* (plural) into the national street design standards. Today the *woonerf*, or a similar form of shared space, is an increasingly accepted traffic-calming measure outside North America, and it is understood by international bodies using standards and engineering practices based on common professional practice.

The Dutch *woonerf*—a street that accommodates pedestrians, bicyclists, and people recreating, in addition to cars—was first developed by residents who took it upon themselves to slow traffic in their neighborhood. (Dick van Veen)

The international acceptance of the *woonerf* demonstrates how unsanctioned, grassroots activity can become sanctioned by bodies of government over time. We introduced this idea—the way unsanctioned innovation leads to sanctioned practice—in chapter 1 and we'll return to it frequently because it demonstrates the importance of allowing bottom-up initiatives to inform the direction of top-down processes.

THE *CASTRA*

Tactical Urbanism is able to scale up when governments choose to facilitate the principles of quick and efficient urban development. The creation of the urban street grid and the resulting block pattern is one strategy used historically in centralized, top-down planning efforts to provide a framework for collective, bottom-up urbanization.

One of the most well-known historical examples of this process is the establishment of the Roman *castra*. Latin for "great legionary encampment," *castra* was the term used for sites reserved for marching and for both temporary and permanent military camps. The Roman historian Flavius described it this way:

As soon as they have marched into an enemy's land, they do not begin to fight till they have walled their camp about; nor is the fence they raise rashly made, or uneven; nor do they all abide in it, nor do those that are in it take their places at random; but if it happens that the ground is uneven, it is first leveled: their camp is also four-square by measure, and carpenters are ready, in great numbers, with their tools, to erect their buildings for them.[7]

Some permanent stone buildings were built for special uses, but the barracks in the camps were first built with temporary materials such as cloth (at least in places with temperate climates such as Spain). Between periods of fighting, the camps morphed into centers of commerce and trade for local inhabitants, and over time the temporary structures gave way to more permanent construction. From Barcelona to Carthage, cities around Europe and the Middle East originated as temporary Roman military camps created with a pattern of easily navigable gridded streets.[8] London, one of the most well-known examples, was initially settled as a *castra* around a.d. 43. The Romans invaded England and traveled inland until they reached the Thames River. Here they built a temporary wooden bridge, east of the present London Bridge. Over time, the bridge, and the framework established by the *castra*, attracted settlers and led to the eventual growth of the city.

THE EVOLUTION OF THE GRID

One of the legacies of the Roman *castra* was the use of the grid as a way to encourage speedy land development.[9] This adaptable and predicable urban growth strategy became the de facto pattern for urban settlements throughout history, from the towns developed under the Laws of the Indies, to colonial era American cities such as Savannah and Philadelphia.

When William Penn laid out a utopian town for Philadelphia in 1682, he used a grid of streets and blocks between the Delaware and Schuylkill Rivers. His original vision was for a "greene Country Towne" of eighty 1-acre "gentleman's estates" with mansions surrounded by fields and gardens spread evenly between the two rivers. Yet Penn was repeatedly rebuffed, because there was no government to enforce the taxes he wanted to levy to pay for the plan. As one account states, "Because the Council met very infrequently, and because no officials had any power to act in the interim, during these intervals Pennsylvania had almost no government at all—and seemed not to suffer from the experience."[10]

In less than 20 years, the city grew into a thriving commercial center despite the lack of government, and over time the city's landowners did not develop mansions on 1-acre lots but instead preferred the more economical, dense pattern of mixed-use development with attached townhouses and narrow interior streets that was not dissimilar from the urbanism many had known in London.[11]

Perhaps the first example of this emergent pattern was the construction of Elfreth's Alley, considered by some to be the nation's oldest continuously inhabited residential street. In 1702, colonial blacksmiths John Gilbert and Arthur Wells, who owned adjacent lots along the river, each ceded a portion of his lot to build a street along their property line in order to connect their smithies near the river with Second Street, a thoroughfare that connected the growing city with points north, west, and beyond.[12] This example of semi-anarchistic, collaborative, peer-to-peer urban development was a response to practical needs and could be considered an early example of citizen-led interventions in America, one that is hard to imagine in the cul-de-sacs of today's suburbia.

THE NORTH AMERICAN BUNGALOW

We have shown that a number of block-scale strategies can help facilitate the creation of citizen-led, fine-grained urbanism, but what about individual buildings? How have our edifices been created by either temporary, centralized planning efforts or permanent, citizen-led land development?

In the early twentieth century, urban growth pressure and the need for accompanying infrastructure (streets, sewer, power, transportation) created a market for real estate developers to subdivide large tracts of land at the edge of a city. The trend marked a shift in the way urban property was developed and was made possible by the emergence of convenient, privately built streetcar lines that gave future residents access to the downtown employment base. The emergent neighborhoods were master planned at one time and included building lots for tightly packed single-family homes, apartments, and accessible retail, set within a grid pattern that mixed rectilinear and curvilinear streets and blocks. The American streetcar suburb was born, as was the era of developer-led urbanization.

One of the many homes available by mail order from the Sears Roebuck Catalog in 1921. ("SearsHome2013" by Sears, Roebuck & Co. Sears Roebuck Catalog, 1921. Licensed under public domain via Wikimedia Commons)

The streetcar suburb developer was not unlike those we know today, but the development framework was very different because it allowed citizens to participate more directly in the growth of their neighborhoods by building catalogue-bought bungalow cottages and homes. For about $1,200 in 1927 (about $15,000 today), a family could buy a set of detailed blueprints that came with a construction manual, and within 2 weeks the materials were shipped so that they could build their homes. The developers did not build the house; they built the infrastructure around the house and sold the land. Because this system predated the full-scale adoption of municipal zoning and land development regulation, there were few bureaucratic hurdles to jump, which kept costs lower for everyone. Indeed, new homeowners did not need to navigate a web of municipal processes or hire an architect, zoning attorney, and contractors to build themselves an attractive house in short order.[13]

The Craftsman catalogues were filled with hundreds of plan variations so that customizable homes could be made appropriate for California as easily as for upstate New York. The Aladdin housing company boasted that anyone who could swing a hammer could build an Aladdin Home.[14] Sears's famous mail-order Modern Home program gave customers the freedom to build their own dream homes with high-quality custom design and favorable financing. The system proved so popular that from 1908 to 1940 Sears, Roebuck and Co. sold between 70,000 and 75,000 homes.

Craftsman bungalows built within the grid of streetcar suburbs were the preferred neighborhood development tactic of their time because they were easily built, replicable, inexpensive, and therefore scalable. In short, they brought a broader neighborhood development plan to life quickly.[15]

In many ways, the proliferation of mail-order houses as an urban tactic can be seen as the predecessor to the global distribution of today's contemporary tactical interventions disseminated through online how-to manuals, guides, and YouTube videos. Well-organized information about Park(ing) Day, chair bombing, open streets, parklets, and other citizen-initiated tactics is easily accessible on the Internet, a tool that was unavailable to previous generations. The surge of interest in shipping-container construction today also takes its cue from this early twentieth-century example of cheap but easily customizable and built urban fabric.

THE WORLD'S FAIR

On the other end of the spectrum of buildings that reflect Tactical Urbanist values are large-scale temporary structures and monuments, such as those that result from the World's Fairs. The built legacy of many of these events is not in the large-scale development that characterizes them but in the public spaces and buildings that they leave behind, which form part of the current fabric of cities such as Paris, New York, Chicago, and St. Louis.

Initiated in 1851 and still active today, the World's Fair, or World's Exposition, is a public exposition hosted by a different city every few years that contains an ensemble of exhibition pavilions, monuments, and cultural activities. The expos can last from 2 to 6 months and showcase cultural, commercial, and technological assets from different countries within a large temporary urban framework built by the host country. And in the world before the Internet, the World's Fair was seen by its participants as an important way to convey cultural, commercial, and technological information on a global scale.

The many World's Fair sites became the testing grounds for top-down urban experimentation by government. It is one of the only instances, besides the Olympic Games, in which a government is allowed to spend untold sums of money on temporary architecture and urbanism. In the context of using short-term action to create long-term change, it's not the expositions themselves that are relevant to the discussion of Tactical Urbanism but the urgency to get things done quickly that forces the construction of buildings, infrastructure, parks, and monuments that often lead to lasting improvements.

One of the most well-known examples is the Eiffel Tower, built for the Exposition Universelle in Paris in 1889. What is now considered an international symbol for French culture and Parisian urban life was intended to be a temporary installation highlighting technological advancements in the use of iron. Similar landmarks with staying power include the Seattle Space Needle (1962) and the Queens Unisphere (1964).

Among the most influential World's Fairs was the 1893 Columbian World Exposition in Chicago. The exposition was held in 1893 to commemorate the 400th anniversary of the arrival of Christopher Columbus in the New World. The fair covered more than 600 acres in Jackson Park and the Midway Plaisance and was designed by some of the nation's greatest planners, architects, and landscape architects, including Daniel Burnham, Louis Sullivan,

George B. Post, Richard Morris Hunt, and Frederick Law Olmsted. In the mind of Daniel Burnham, the lead architect and planner, it was the grand prototype of what a city could be.

Approximately 200 temporary buildings designed in the Beaux-Arts style were constructed with wood, covered with white stucco, and lined with the recent innovation of alternate-current lightbulbs, which when illuminated at night gave the exposition its moniker "The White City." More than 27 million people attended the fair during the 6 months that it was open, the numbers second only to the Exposition Universelle in Paris, which was open a full 6 months longer. Some proposed making the buildings permanent, but a fire on the fairgrounds in 1894 cut the expo short. Although most of the buildings were lost, many physical improvements made to the grounds were lasting, most notably a redesigned and expanded Jackson Park.

It was written that the "White City represented itself as a representation, an admitted sham. Yet that sham, it insisted, held a truer vision of the real than did the troubled world sprawling beyond its gates."[16] And it is in the lasting influence on the world of architecture and city planning beyond Jackson Park where the expo finds its true legacy. To be sure, the power of this temporary city catalyzed the City Beautiful movement and the modern city planning profession as we know it by exhibiting how planners, landscape architects, and architects could collaboratively compose a setting for public life. The White City motivated cities the world over to beautify their streets, commission municipal art, and create public spaces and public buildings. It is one of history's definitive demonstration projects.[17]

Urban Rituals in Public Spaces

We have discussed examples of tactical approaches to large-scale city building activities: grids, streets, and buildings. Now we want to shift focus to the programming that happens in these spaces involving recreation, art, civic participation, and commerce. The instigators of these activities are wide ranging, from citizens, to fraternal orders, to municipal and regional governments, yet all involve mobile or temporary activities that activate public space.[18]

2.1 San Diego's Balboa Park

Another notable example of the long-term influence of the World's Fair on a host city is found in San Diego's Balboa Park. Created in 1865, the park was improved on when it was chosen as the site of the 1915 Panama–California Exposition, and again with the 1935 California Pacific International Exposition. Notable among these improvements are the Cabrillo Bridge connecting the park with the surrounding street network, the design of many formal gardens and public spaces by Frank Lloyd Wright, and dozens of public buildings and pavilions that still exist today.

In anticipation of the centennial celebration of the 1915 Panama–California Exposition, a new master plan was drafted for the park in 2011. A key recommendation called for restoring the Plaza de Panama in front of the San Diego Museum into a true pedestrian plaza. For years the plaza was used as a large surface parking lot, marring the heart of the otherwise great civic space. To maintain parking supply, the plan called for the construction of a new parking garage in addition to other park upgrades.

Faced with political and legal challenges, the controversial $45 million project was tabled in favor of a cheaper, iterative approach estimated to cost 1 percent as much. Because the parking was not thought to be crucial in the near term, the city painted the ground

LEFT (top): The Plaza de Panama was used as a large surface parking lot for years. (Howard Blackson)

LEFT (bottom): Abandoning a much more costly long-term plan, the City of San Diego turned the Plaza de Panama into a true pedestrian plaza using low-cost materials. (Howard Blackson)

an attractive light tan color, put out some planters, and committed to seeing what would happen. Motorists could still circulate slowly through one part of the reclaimed plaza, but the integrity of this formerly grand public space was almost instantly restored. Capturing the spirit of Tactical Urbanism, the city's former mayor said at the time, "If a certain element doesn't work the city can try something else."[a]

Despite some initial controversy over the potential impact on park and museum attendance, the conversion of the plaza led to record-setting attendance at the Timken Museum. The result has been a resounding success according to city planners, with residents demanding even more programming for the space. The city is pursuing plans for a scaled-back centennial celebration, with new lighting around the plaza, while the permanent redesign is on hold.

---

a. Lisa Halverstadt, "Inspiration for Plaza de Panama: Bryant Park, Zócalo and Red Square," Voice of San Diego, July 29, 2013, http://voiceofsandiego.org/2013/07/29/inspiration-for-plaza -de-panama-bryant-park-zocalo-and-red-square/. See also Gene Cubbinson, "Parking Lot Removed in Plaza de Panama," NBC San Diego, June 10, 2013, http://www.nbcsandiego .com/news/local/Parking-Lot-Removed-in-Plaza-de-Panama -Balboa-Park-210837961.html; Lauren Steussy, "Timeline: Plaza de Panama," NBC San Diego, June 10, 2013, http://www .nbcsandiego.com/news/politics/Timeline-Plaza-de-Panama -138954679.html.

PLAY STREETS

Street fairs and bazaars, markets, block parties, and similar temporary events have brought life to streets for millennia, proving that our thoroughfares fulfill a rich social and economic purpose as much as a utilitarian one. Unfortunately, in the early 1900s the nascent traffic engineering profession, automobile manufacturers, oil producers, and insurance companies collectively hijacked our streets for a century of relentless motoring. Yet almost as soon as cars began dominating urban streets, tactical interventions were organized to take them back, even if only temporarily.

At the dawn of the motoring age, crowded conditions and the lack of urban park space meant that streets were the principal place of play for children and the primary social space for adults. The introduction of the automobile to city streets clashed with this culture and quickly led to a spike in child fatalities, among other maladies. The idea of creating temporary play streets—closing a few blocks to automobile traffic so that kids could play safely—emerged from police departments as a tactic to keep children safe in urban centers such as New York and London.

In 1909, the *New York Times* reported that the city's police commissioner had drafted a plan for a pilot project to regulate traffic for the protection of pedestrians, particularly children (not dissimilar from the pilot projects cities implement today). The New York City Parks and Playgrounds Association helped design the program to "be of mutual benefit to drivers and pedestrians" by prohibiting traffic during after-school hours on certain blocks "where the population is the thickest." Children were able to have a safe area to play while leaving neighboring blocks clear for "both carters and chauffeurs" to drive.[19]

The new pilot program took into consideration such factors as whether businesses would be hurt by the street closing, whether the street had a large number of tenements or residents, and whether the traffic was favorably light (38 wagons every 5 minutes or 25 automobiles an hour was considered heavy traffic). The *New York Times* read,

> While a hot, asphalted, treeless block does not make a beautiful playground, with the carting barred after school hours, they would at least be safe and inexpensive and clear the neighboring streets of the youngsters. If trees could be planted on those same selected blocks in the congested neighborhoods, the advocates of this new traffic regulation

scheme believe that a practical way of securing adequate play space at very little cost will have been found.

Indeed, the temporary repurposing of the street proved to be a very quick and low-cost method to maintain the recreation areas and outdoor play spaces for neighborhood youth while also reclaiming the social life of neighborhoods.

Building from the success of the early pilot projects, the New York City Police Athletic League established a summer play streets program in 1914, which included supervised areas for children to play sports and games and take part in cultural activities. Police commissioner Arthur Woods set aside twenty-nine city blocks in Manhattan where traffic was prohibited in the afternoons on every day except Sunday. In 1916, a New York City police officer, in defense of play streets, told the *New York Times*, "It is only natural that children should want to play and if the city refuses to provide playgrounds for them, they are going to play in the streets." The same article reported that the objective of the play streets was to "reduce the temptations of wrongdoings by keeping children off the streets and by giving them a chance for wholesome play under proper supervision." Because of the success and scalability of the initial program, twenty-five play streets were created by 1921, and another fifty were added in Brooklyn, the Bronx, and Queens soon thereafter.

Despite their popularity, play streets programs in New York City and elsewhere nearly went extinct with rising automobile use and suburbanization. However, today they have reemerged as a tool to combat the negative impacts cars have on our cities. However, this time around concerned citizens are often leading the effort. In England, which once had hundreds of play street programs patterned after those found in New York City in the early twentieth century, citizen-led efforts have led to policy changes.

For example, in 2011 a group of concerned parents in Bristol, England appropriated legislation designed for street parties to close their street to cars so that their children could play safely.[20] Within months, the Bristol City Council recognized the benefits and introduced a new policy allowing residents to close streets to traffic for up to 3 hours a week for children's play. The effort led to a grant from the Department of Health, and the parents-turned-community-leaders established a national advocacy organization called Playing Out, which offers consultation to parents who want to

Building from the success of the early pilot projects, the New York City Police Athletic League established a summer play streets program in 1914, which included supervised car-free areas for children to play sports and games and take part in cultural activities. (Courtesy NYC Municipal Archives, NYPD & Criminal Prosecution Collection)

establish play streets in their own neighborhoods.[21] Two years later Bristol boasted more than forty play streets, and the tactic is once again spreading to numerous cities throughout England.

And in the United States, with support from First Lady Michelle Obama's Partnership for a Healthy America, play streets are being used to encourage physical activity and help combat the growing epidemic of childhood obesity. (See chapter 4 for a more detailed discussion of New York City's most successful, citizen-led play streets initiative.)

OPENING STREETS, TRANSFORMING COMMUNITIES

Newer in concept, open streets initiatives could be considered the expansion of the play streets movement. Not to be confused with block parties, street fairs, or similar events, open streets initiatives, such as the Ciclovía initiative in Bogotá, Colombia, mentioned in the preface, temporarily close

streets to automobiles so that people may use them for healthy and fun physical activities such as walking, jogging, biking, and dancing. According to
Gil Peñalosa, executive director of Toronto-based 8–80 Cities and former
commissioner of parks for Bogotá, "People traffic replaces car traffic, and
the streets become 'paved parks' where people of all ages, abilities, and
social, economic, or ethnic backgrounds can come out and improve their
mental, physical, and emotional health."

Today, many North American open streets organizers draw inspiration
from Central and South American cities, where Bogotá, Colombia, rolled
out its now-famed Ciclovía ("bike path") in 1974. However, before there
was Ciclovía in Bogotá, there was Seattle Bicycle Sundays, a car-free initiative connecting several parks along a 3-mile stretch of Lake Washington
Boulevard. First launched in 1965, Bicycle Sundays predates Bogotá's initiative by nearly a decade and is North America's oldest open streets event.
Seattle's effort quickly inspired similar initiatives in the parks and parkways
of New York City (1966), San Francisco (1967), and Ottawa (1970), all four
of which still take place today.

A few North American open streets programs were created between the
activism of the 1960s and 1970s and the mid-2000s, but more than 100 open
streets initiatives have been developed in the United States and Canada since
2006. Open streets are typically part of a broader city or organizational effort
to encourage sustained physical activity, increase community engagement,
and build support for the provision of nonmotorized transportation choices.
These unique objectives distinguish open streets from play streets and help
participants see and connect with their community in a whole new way.

Both play streets and open streets show the important role citizens have
played in using a city's primary form of open space, the street. We believe
that supporting and proactively engaging people in a way that emboldens
this type of street-scale activity is one of the more important tasks for modern
governance and planning. Through the adoption of policy and project development, municipal leaders are in a position to use their limited resources to
scale the best bottom-up initiatives citywide. For city and citizen, Tactical
Urbanism is now *the* primary tool for doing so.

BONNIE ORA SHERK AND THE BIRTH OF PARKMAKING

The creative, temporary adaptation of streets is also found in the history of

Bogotá, Colombia, rolled out its famed Ciclovía ("bike path") in 1974, closing certain streets off to auto traffic temporarily. Ciclovía is still practiced in Bogotá today. (Photo by Pedro Felipe. Accessed via Wikimedia Commons)

parklets, the microparks now colonizing parking spaces in a city near you (see chapter 4). Although these small-scale and sometimes seasonal pop-up parks are viewed as a contemporary tactic for reclaiming public space, they can be traced to the work of Bonnie Ora Sherk, a San Francisco and New York City–based artist and landscape architect.

In the early 1970s Sherk developed a series of art installations in San Francisco that provided commentary on the allocation and use of public space. At this time, park space in America's cities was suffering from severe disinvestment, partially because of the reduced tax base that resulted from the exodus to the suburbs. For Sherk, the motive was to use art to make people think differently about public space. "It was the first public project using performance art to explore how to change the city," Sherk told us over coffee at a West Village café. Her most well-known intervention of this type, titled *Portable Architecture*, began in 1970 and should be considered the forerunner of pop-up parks and Park(ing) Day installations found in cities across the globe. Her incredibly prescient interventions, which repurposed automobile infrastructure into temporary parks, foreshadowed a theme in urbanism that would gain widespread notoriety 35 years later.

Sherk's original *Portable Architecture* installations revealed the potential for artists to inspire infrastructure improvements but also illustrated that the arts in general were missing from the planning and implementation process.

Supported by a $1,000 grant from the San Francisco Museum of Art, Sherk designed and implemented a series of portable parks at three locations in San Francisco over the span of 4 days. The installations were located on top of and below freeway on-ramps and on Maiden Lane in downtown San Francisco. They included whimsical elements such as farm animals (borrowed from the city's zoo), palm trees, thick sod, and benches, which "had the startling impact of real life Magrittean mirages."[22] Part art and part protest, the intervention was not only ahead of its time but representative of the practice of resistance that also informed the nascent Bay Area culture of hacking that gave rise to personal computing.

"Bonnie Ora Sherk's first public artwork temporarily revitalized the dead, mechanistic urban spaces of San Francisco through 'bucolic demonstrations' in the form of portable parks featuring plants and animals," said curator Tanya Zimbardo. As with public space interventions today, the onus was on Sherk to find sites for these installations and obtain the necessary permits. "With the Portable Parks it was necessary for me to deal with certain established systems, communicate with them, and convince them of the rightness of the work," she told us. And when we inquired about how she dealt with city's response to her project, Sherk explained that because it was unusual at the time, there were no protocols in place to say "no." She merely had to obtain an "encroachment permit" from Caltrans to place a portable park on top of and below the freeway, a task that would not be so simple today.[23]

A recent resurgence of interest in 1970s interventions such as Sherk's has coincided with a growing focus among a new generation of artists on temporary installations that fuse environmentalism and urban planning to demonstrate how temporary public art installations can inspire improvements to infrastructure.[24]

RIGHT: Bonnie Ora Sherk, a San Francisco and New York City–based artist and landscape architect, developed a series of public space installations in San Francisco in the early 1970s that provided commentary on the city's lack of green space. (Bonnie Ora Sherk)

Along with the other examples in this section, Sherk's temporary parks made a strong statement about how we use streets and value open space. In the following examples, we'll describe how small-scale mobile activities, either for civic participation or commerce, can have a big impact on how public spaces are used.

MOBILE LIBRARIES

From city hall to municipal libraries, public services have existed in mobile form throughout history. Whereas today's mobile libraries take shape as trucks, vans, or buses, past iterations include bicycle, wagon, donkey cart, camel, motorbike, boat, helicopter, and train. No matter the mode, each relied on both the stewardship of a top-down entity—a municipality, nonprofit organization, or in some cases wealthy individuals—and the citizens who patronized the services provided.

Some of the earliest examples of mobile libraries were developed in Victorian England. In the Cumberland region, philanthropist George Moore started a mobile pushcart library, which traveled between eight different towns dropping off and picking up books. Consistent with Victorian ideals of self-improvement and social mobility, an article from this era describes the best practices associated with the mobile library so that others could "diffuse good literature among the rural population." [25] Another early example, from 1858, involved the Mechanics Institute of Warrington, England. The institute organized a "perambulating library" with a subscription service for working-class men who paid a small fee in order to bring education to those who could not otherwise afford it. The van, horse, and books cost £275, and more than 12,000 books were borrowed in the first year.

In the United States, the tradition of mobile libraries began at the turn of the nineteenth century. Librarian Mary L. Titcomb from Maryland's Washington County organized the installation of twenty-three small-scale libraries in post offices and retail stores around the county. Each "branch" had fifty books and the ability to lend books and accept returns from other branches. This effort was followed by a mobile book delivery service that eventually reached every corner of the rural county via a horse-drawn buggy with books from the Hagerstown, Maryland Public Library. Titcomb described the scene this way:

The Warrington Perambulating Library, illustrated in an 1860 edition of *The Illustrated London News*. (Public domain. Accessed via Wikimedia Commons)

The first wagon, when finished with shelves on the outside and a place for storage of cases in the center resembled somewhat a cross between a grocer's delivery wagon and the tin peddlers cart of bygone New England days.[26]

Over time, bookmobiles became a common part of metropolitan library systems across the country, augmenting the reach of brick-and-mortar locations in cities where suburban or rural expansion made building libraries costly. In Miami-Dade County a bookmobile began plying the streets in the 1920s. It was used to serve the far reaches of the county before municipal services could catch up to the region's fast-paced growth.

The mobile library also served an important role after natural disasters. West Kendall Regional Library, close to the western boundary of Miami-Dade County, was only a few months old when Hurricane Andrew hit in 1992. It was located in a suburban strip mall and was completely destroyed. It would not be rebuilt for several years, so in its place came a bookmobile

that served the community between 1992 and 1994, when the rebuilt library was opened.

Today, bookmobiles have evolved alongside the technology and cultural preferences of the day and offer items such as DVDs and Internet workstations. A bookmobile in Memphis, Tennessee offers a mobile job and career center in addition to normal library services. Similarly, the El Paso, Texas Public Library brings Internet technology to one of the poorest counties in the country, where one in three adults are illiterate. The bookmobile allows patrons to conduct job searches, fill out job applications, and attend computer training sessions, a tactic attempting to bring equity and access to needed educational and social services.

There are currently more than 900 mobile libraries in operation around the United States, with many independent (nonmunicipal library)

TOP: In Miami-Dade County a bookmobile began plying the streets in the 1920s. It was used for decades as a way to serve the far reaches of the county before municipal services could catch up to the region's fast-paced growth. (Miami Public Library Mobile, ca. 1954, courtesy of the Miami-Dade Public Library System)

RIGHT: Little Free Library. (Jak Krumholtz)

TOP: The City of Boston has developed "City Hall to Go," a repurposed city SWAT team truck that moves from neighborhood to neighborhood to deliver municipal services. (Photo courtesy of the City of Boston)

bookmobiles gaining momentum and providing a richer array of cultural services. Moreover, even smaller Little Free Libraries are proliferating in towns and cities across the globe, providing a micro, peer-to-peer version of the library where people drop off and pick up books at will. These nano-libraries even have a website dedicated to sharing building plans, similar to the Craftsman catalogue instructions from a century earlier or the contemporary do-it-yourself Internet guides to building furniture out of shipping pallets.

It is not only municipal government that is using the bookmobile model. A Brooklyn-based group called Art House organizes global, collaborative art projects and is traveling across the country with a mobile library. "The ease by which we can set up and interact with the public right on the street makes it so accessible and approachable, which is what we want all our art projects to be. Art House is about creating communities through projects like The Sketchbook Project, and the Mobile Library is the embodiment of that. We can physically drive our collection to your door!"[27]

Today, civic, cultural, and commercial services are being diversified further as the mobile trend accelerates. For example, art sales and fashion trucks may be seen traversing the streets of New York City, Los Angeles, Atlanta, and numerous other American cities. The City of Boston has admirably developed "City Hall to Go," a repurposed city SWAT team truck that moves from neighborhood to neighborhood to deliver municipal services. According to one *Boston Globe* article, the mobile City Hall allows residents to "pay and dispute parking tickets; pay property taxes; register to vote; request birth, marriage, and death certificates; and take advantage of a variety of other services."[28]

Such services push the boundary of municipal government by bringing services to where people already are rather than requiring people to seek out the services they need in an often inconvenient and alienating central location. In addition to providing services, they almost always fill other needs in the community because they temporarily bring more diverse activity to underused space.[29] In much the same way, the commercial activities of both *les bouquinistes* and the century-long evolution of the modern-day food truck exemplify bottom-up activities offering sociocultural benefits for the city and economic opportunities for an aspiring merchant class.

LES BOUQUINISTES

If you've been to Paris you've probably seen hundreds of green wooden boxes perched atop the embankment of the River Seine. Depending on the time of day, you would have witnessed a variety of print media—magazines, books, newspapers, postcards, and the like—spilling out of the boxes in a scene that has come to represent one of the iconic images of contemporary Paris. What most visitors don't know is that these booksellers, called *les bouquinistes*, have been peddling bestsellers since the 1500s. Their presence today represents a 500-year timeline of commercial activity that is now regulated and institutionalized by the City of Paris. However, this wasn't always the case.

Les bouquinistes began selling books out of wheelbarrows along the banks of the Seine, only to later expand to the many bridges around the city. As business improved, the wheelbarrows gave way to small, green stalls that were placed on top of the stone river embankments with leather straps. Their early commercial success did not go unnoticed. As early as 1557, the municipal government categorized many of *les bouquinistes* as thieves because they sold forbidden Protestant pamphlets during the Wars of Religion.[30]

Despite their reputation, *les bouquinistes* occupied many bridges around the city during the seventeenth century, most notably the Pont Neuf, which led to conflicts with the established merchants located nearby, who often chased them from the area. Similar to brick-and-mortar restaurants denouncing today's food trucks, bookstore owners complained loudly enough to have the temporary booksellers banned in 1649. However, these persistent entrepreneurs wouldn't be deterred.

After the French Revolution (1789–1799), the private libraries of many French nobles and clergymen were looted and democratized by *les bouquinistes*, making them more popular than ever.[31] Although their popularity again attracted the ire of storeowners, the city eventually legalized their presence in the 1850s. The new regulations confined them to specific locations, limited their activity to Sundays or holidays when the bookshops were closed, and stipulated that each "shop" must collapse into a box at day's end; *les bouquinistes* were asked to operate a literal pop-up shop.

By the turn of the nineteenth century, they were allowed to permanently attach the boxes to the riverbank, and by 1930 the dimensions of the boxes and the number of licenses issued were standardized. This slow progression from unsanctioned to sanctioned activity shows that a successful model will survive and thrive despite the vicissitudes of municipal politics.

The triumph of *les bouquinistes* may be attributed to their location and consistency. Indeed, as a daily occurrence they became a common if not beloved part of the city's social, economic, and physical fabric. They also illustrate how one of the city's basic rituals—commerce—helps activate public space. Today, the booksellers are exempt from paying property taxes and are given free Seine-side space by the Parisian government. With more than 240 *bouquinistes* and an 8-year waitlist to set up shop, one must assume that business is good. Moreover, since 1992 the little green boxes have been part of a United Nations Educational, Scientific and Cultural Organization (UNESCO) World Heritage site designation for the River Seine, which makes this example one of the slowest, if not the most lauded examples of Tactical Urbanism we've found to date.[32]

FOOD TRUCKS

Among the most popular contemporary commercial rituals and public space activation tactics is the provision of food trucks. Their history in America,

RIGHT: *Les bouquinistes* have been peddling reading materials on Paris's River Seine since the 1500s. (Photo by Keystone-France/Gamma-Keystone via Getty Images, ca. 1900)

ranging from the western chuckwagon of the 1800s to the modern-day food truck with thousands of Twitter followers, cannot be overlooked. Similar to the original incarnation of the traveling *bouquinistes*, mobile food purveyors have the distinct advantage of being able to locate where the need or opportunity is greatest. Of course, street food has existed for thousands of years and remains the most basic bottom-up entrepreneurial activity of the city. Indeed, there are records from as far back as ancient Greek, Roman, and Chinese civilizations of merchants who had animal-drawn food carts. In the New World, there are records from the late seventeenth century of food carts being regulated in New Amsterdam, known today as New York City.

However, the modern version of the food truck can be traced to the 1860s, when a Texas Ranger named Charles Goodnight introduced the chuckwagon, a covered wagon that contained basic necessities for cattlemen as they herded cattle in the remote parts of the American West. On the road for months at a time, camping in isolated locations with no other options for food preparation or storage, cattlemen needed foods that were easy to preserve, such as coffee, cornmeal, dried beans, and salted meats. The chuckwagons also included provisions such as tables, utensils, spices, first aid supplies, and a sling for kindling, which allowed cattlemen to cook food. The chuckwagon also served a social purpose for the nomadic cattlemen, who had no other physical framework around which to gather after work: The chuckwagon provided a location for cattlemen to congregate and form a community.

The chuckwagon was a nimble response serving those needing access to convenient food and provisions while working or traveling in remote areas. The rise of food trucks in urban areas was a similar response, albeit for an entirely different context. In the 1870s, late-night food options were almost nonexistent in urban areas. Seeing a market that wasn't being catered to, newspaperman Walter Scott of Providence, Rhode Island developed a freight wagon that housed a diner. Known as the "first restaurant on wheels," the horse-drawn diner was stationed outside the *Providence Journal* offices and sold prepared food to workers on the night shift and patrons of nearby gentlemen's clubs (or anyone out between dusk and dawn).[33]

Like the chuckwagon, Scott's diner is also considered an early predecessor of the modern food truck and is widely believed to be the first diner in the United States, a catalyst for the workaday lunch car and diner movement that

Cowboys eating in front of a chuckwagon, ca. 1880–1910. (Public domain. Accessed via the Library of Congress)

swept through most of America. Not surprisingly, other lunch and late-night dinner wagons began popping up, including the Henry Ford Night Owl Lunch Wagon in Greenfield, Michigan[34] and Haven Brothers in Providence, which dates back to 1888 and can still be seen serving patrons on Kennedy Plaza today.[35]

The rubber-tired, gas-guzzling food trucks that we all know and love today originated in the early 1900s and soon replaced most horse-drawn carts. Between 1900 and 1960 food trucks became a fixture in American cities and suburbs, from the familiar Good Humor ice cream truck or the Oscar Mayer "Wienermobile" to less well-known examples such as the mobile hot waffle carts of New Orleans. The rising popularity of food trucks, similar to the experience of *les bouquinistes*, was not without tension from restaurateurs who feared competition and municipal governments that didn't know quite how to regulate them.

Haven Brothers today, in Providence, RI. (Mike Lydon)

Municipal governments worked to regulate and control the growth of the food truck and mobile food phenomena. Officials in Los Angeles initially tried to ban food carts in the 1890s, only to find their popularity boom. The city soon changed course, choosing tighter regulations rather than outright prohibition by requiring that they close at a reasonable hour because they attracted late-night revelers as the bars closed down. One article from the *Los Angeles Times* described how the city's robust street food scene looked to outsiders. "Strangers coming to Los Angeles remark at the presence of so many outdoor restaurants, and marvel at the system which permits men ... to set up places of business in the public streets ... competing with businessmen who pay high rents for rooms in which to serve the public with food."[36]

As American culinary tastes expanded, so did the offerings of food trucks. In Los Angeles, Mexican immigrants began bringing their culinary traditions to California in the late 1800s. With scarce resources they opted for the low-cost and more nimble mobile version of a brick-and-mortar restaurant.

Although many urban food trucks have offered Mexican fare historically in Los Angeles, Raul Martinez, who is considered the father of the city's thriving taco truck ecosystem, best exemplifies the path to success. In 1974 Martinez converted an ice cream truck into a taco truck and parked it outside an East Los Angeles bar. He was so successful that it took him only 6 months to establish his first Taco King restaurant location. By 1987, he had built a mini restaurant empire with $10 million in sales, in addition to three 40-foot taco trucks and ten taco stands that helped him reach markets all over Los Angeles.[37]

The Taco King once again demonstrates how Tactical Urbanism is as much an economic development engine as a paradigm for urban planning and placemaking; the low start-up cost of the food truck allows entrepreneurs to get a foothold in the market, allowing them to bypass the economic and regulatory burdens of the conventional restaurant business while they grow a customer base. This reality was on full view in the post-recession food truck boom, which was sparked by a glut of recently laid-off gourmet chefs and failed restaurant owners who found a market for their skills in the food truck business and nearly instant followings via Twitter. Their success in this low-entry-barrier business afforded many of them the opportunity to enter the brick-and-mortar business once the economy improved, just as Raul Martinez did decades previously.[38] Ironically, the economic forces of the Great Recession also saw the reverse of this trend: brick-and-mortar restaurants expanding into the food truck market as a way of augmenting weak sales and reaching new locations without heavy infrastructure costs.

Municipal ordinances governing food trucks are less onerous than those governing brick-and-mortar restaurants, yet food trucks still face regulatory burdens. Regulations were used either to try to eliminate competition for brick-and-mortar restaurants or, in contemporary times, as a matter of public health and hygiene. Some of these regulations are necessary, but others are remnants of a fast-disappearing era. For instance, in Chicago food trucks are not allowed to park within 200 feet of a restaurant or stay for more than 2 hours at a particular location.[39] Today, there are food truck associations around the country actively working to repeal such out-of-date laws, which were designed to make vending difficult. This example once again underscores the tension that rises when government regulations struggle to keep pace with changing trends and cultural preferences.

Food trucks have long been a cheap and easy alternative for those looking for food: ice cream trucks catering to children who can't drive and night owls catering to the midnight crowd when all other options go dark. But beyond these basic needs, it is their ability to create social activity and attract people to one location that make them a reliable tactic for activating otherwise moribund urban spaces. From the time of the chuckwagon to today, people want to be in spaces where there are other people. When public spaces fail because they lack the necessary framework to facilitate human activity, food trucks often provide just the spark needed to bring them back to life, if only for a few hours a day.[40]

SEASIDE, FLORIDA: A TACTICAL (NEW) URBANISM

From citizens building and maintaining the first urban street to the triumph of *les bouquinistes*, low-cost, mobile, temporary, and even unsanctioned responses to the issues of the day have the potential to be widely adopted and highly influential, at the macro or micro scale. As our final example shows, when both the framework and rituals come together, great places can be made.

First tested in the rural scrub pineland of the Florida panhandle, the New Urbanism was critical of modernist planning theory and practice and was able to translate its principles into a viable alternative to the top-down cocktail of federal, state, and local regulations that mandated a suburban sprawl life-style (more on this in chapter 3). Its theories and practice of compact, walkable urbanism were first tested in the coastal community of Seaside in the early 1980s, in much the same way that the White City tested City Beautiful theories nearly a century earlier. The 80-acre community was incubated with temporary structures and programming demonstrating New Urbanist principles. Indeed, town founders Robert and Daryl Davis shunned modern practices by approaching the development of Seaside in a slow, phased way that not only was consistent with a beach lifestyle but exemplifies how developers can use Tactical Urbanism to seed long-term development, even in a very remote location. As Robert Davis would say, "Seaside would thus grow slowly, one street at a time."

Although the Davises had a great conceptual plan for their ideal town, the pace of development ensured that they could test out the market before taking the master plan beyond the conceptual stage. They initially built a beach pavilion and two houses; both were used as sales models, and one was also their house. "It was Daryl's advice, in 1981, to stop trying to design the perfect vernacular beach cottage for Northwest Florida and build one or two

RIGHT (top): An underused vacant lot in Brooklyn's DUMBO neighborhood. (Mike Lydon)

RIGHT (bottom): Beginning in 2013, the same vacant lot was enlivened five times a week by food trucks. (Mike Lydon)

Seaside Saturday Market, ca. 1982. (Image courtesy of the Seaside Archives and the Seaside Research Portal at the University of Notre Dame, seaside.library.nd.edu)

that seemed pretty good. Just as one 'practiced' architecture, one could 'practice' development, refining and improving over time." Once again, the use of an iterative process is at the heart of Tactical Urbanism: build, measure, learn, repeat.

In a similar way, the Davises also relied on programming within their budding community to catalyze interest and attract people to the community. Daryl would set up a projector for impromptu movie nights in the town square. Seaside's commercial core started as an open air market under canvas tents where people sold fruits and vegetables, handcrafts, and flea market items long before any permanent structures were built, in a manner similar to the markets that formed the commercial beginnings of London, Philadelphia, or other temporary settlements mentioned earlier.

Daryl Davis later said, "Our Saturday Market turned into stores and restaurants and our events became major attractions. And it all began with some ingenuity, the dream of a better way of life, and a little veggie stand.

I can't say we planned for this to happen, and I can't say that we didn't. We both were very interested in creating activities in Seaside and from those first attempts at community building our retail enterprise slowly began and flourished."[41]

Seaside is a classic example of New Urbanism, yet it used Tactical Urbanism in its infancy. Whereas New Urbanism focuses largely on the intersection of policy and physical form as a necessary progenitor of a healthier economy, environment, and populace, Tactical Urbanism adds the elements of program and ritual into the use and adaptation of new and existing physical spaces.[42] The revelation is that simply defining and designing beautiful public space is not enough. Ritual and use have to be further instigated; without the programming and activities—*the rituals of daily life*—that take place in public space there can be no urban life.

03 THE NEXT AMERICAN CITY AND THE RISE OF TACTICAL URBANISM

—

Although we haven't yet realized it, our societies are on the cusp of a transformation as dramatic as the one the Athenians wrought when they decided to elect leaders instead of choosing them by birthright. We have a tremendous opportunity to reimagine the kind of society we want to live in and bring it into being.

—NICCO MELE
The End of Big

The recent rise of Tactical Urbanism in North America is underpinned by four major trends and events: people moving back to the city, the Great Recession, the rapid rise of the Internet, and the growing disconnect between government and citizens. Taken together they expose the need for cities to not just reform how they work but to change the kind of work they are set up to perform. The cities that have begun to respond to these needs are already out ahead and have begun to define the evolution of the Next American City.

A Renewed Love Affair with the City

Cities are as central to human civilization as they've ever been, and increasingly more so. One hundred years ago, 2 out of every 10 people around the world lived in an urban area. By 2010, more than half of us lived in urban areas, and it's predicted that by 2050 this proportion will increase to 7 out of 10.[1] As impressive as these numbers are, they don't tell the entire story because the shift to living in cities has been accompanied by an exponential growth

63

Four converging trends and events have helped increase the use of Tactical Urbanism interventions.

in the global population. Both the scale and the speed of global urbanization have created an urgent need to deliver fast, low-cost, and high-impact urban improvements, particularly in contexts where resources are perpetually strained.

More than four out of five Americans live in metropolitan regions, a term that broadly defines the exurbs, suburbs, and the downtowns they rely on. Our core cities are surrounded by rings of suburbs, some with their own commercial nodes and downtowns of varying vintage. Some of these are intentionally becoming more like the core city each year: dense, walkable, and transit-served. Others have little to no interest in developing these urban characteristics and may be viewed as stalwarts of an era when the conditions of the city were not looked at favorably.

Today, foot-, bike-, and transit-friendly communities are drawing in two major demographic cohorts: the Millennial generation (those roughly between the ages of 18 and 35), often referred to as Generation Y, and, to a lesser extent, those born in the post–World War II era, commonly referred to as the Baby Boomers. Both are converging on places that offer commercial, cultural, and recreational amenities that are accessible in a variety of ways.

This is a big deal. Eighty million Millennials—the largest generational cohort in American history—desiring a different type of living arrangement are having a big impact on the spatial layout of our cities. Millennials marry and start families much later than previous generations, perform more freelance work, start their own businesses at higher rates, and are generally attracted to urban environments where car-free or "car-lite" lifestyles are possible. A 2012 article in *The Atlantic* explored these trends further, noting, "Since World War II, new cars and suburban houses have powered the economy and propelled recoveries. Millennials may have lost interest in both."[2]

Brooklyn Love. (Mike Lydon)

These young adults are moving to cities where transportation options are plentiful and are less likely to get a driver's license than previous generations by nearly 30 percent, a trend mirrored by data on car ownership, which has dropped by one third for the 18- to 32-year-old demographic since 1980.

These trends are having a noticeable impact on our driving habits. An ongoing University of Michigan study titled "Has Motorization in the U.S. Peaked?" reveals that it's not just Millennials who are less interested in driving. The study shows that per capita driving actually peaked in 2004, years before the Great Recession. This study and others like it assert that although it's a little early to tell, a sustained reduction in vehicle miles traveled, car purchases, and gasoline consumption may be here to stay.[3]

Early evidence suggests that an overwhelming number of these young adults will prefer staying in walkable urban locations or at least move to older walkable suburbs rather than areas where housing is cheaper but getting around is more expensive (one-quarter of a typical suburban family's budget now goes to transportation).[4]

These shifts are exciting in many ways, but they continue to expose disconnects between the cities we have and the kind of cities we want. Indeed, many American cities are working under philosophical approaches, regulatory structures, public involvement processes, and infrastructure programs that were established in response to the demographic, economic, and sociocultural trends of another era.

More specifically, our city's zoning codes and land use ordinances still skew toward low-density patterns of growth favoring a single mode of transportation: the automobile. Dozens of books, studies, and plans routinely point to billions of dollars spent under the various Federal Highway and Transportation Acts, dating back as far as the Roosevelt era, as a major factor producing suburban sprawl. That may be true, but the top-down, citizenless approach to building the Interstate system through healthy, functional urban neighborhoods was far more damaging to the American city than any sprawl subsidy.

Of course, helpful regulatory patches and tools have been created over the years: zoning overlay districts, performance zoning, planned unit developments, and form-based codes at the local level and the landmark Intermodal Surface Transportation Efficiency Act and HOPE VI at the federal level. These call for improvements to the status quo yet are too often grafted onto a

The Millennial and car-free mayor Svante Myrick (sporting the tie) walks to work, so he transformed his prime Ithaca City Hall parking space into a parklet and edited the sign to read, "Reserved for Mayor … And Friends." (Svante Myrick/Facebook)

broken and increasingly bankrupt system, one that is not designed for today's challenges and opportunities, let alone those we'll face in the future. With an ongoing and still urgent need to update the project delivery system, we wonder who's up for the challenge.

Cities that continue on this path will find it tough to compete regionally, nationally, and even internationally. And with 80 percent of Americans now living in urbanized areas, overcoming this challenge—one that is seemingly hidden in plain sight—will require a different approach to building and regulating the American city.[5]

For many the arrival of the New Urbanism in the 1980s was a beacon of progressive planning. New Urbanism was started by a small group of architects who saw the traditional pattern of compact, walkable urbanism as a solution to the effects of suburban sprawl on the American city. By 1996, the articulation of twenty-seven core principles—from the scale of the building to that of the region—eschewed the results of the suburban experiment and projected a clear alternative: walkable urbanity. So compelling was the vision

Many urban highways ripped through functioning neighborhoods when constructed. Pictured here is the interchange of Arroyo Seco Parkway and Highway 101, in Los Angeles County, CA. (Public domain. Accessed via Wikimedia Commons)

that in 1996 *New York Times* architectural critic Herbert Muschamp called New Urbanism "the most important phenomenon to emerge in American architecture in the post–Cold War era."[6]

New Urbanism repudiated the ahistorical character of modernism and derided its perspective that cities were something to be viewed and experienced from a car or plane and that buildings were separate objects needing very little relationship to their cultural and physical surroundings. The early victory of the New Urbanism was in shifting the academic and professional conversation away from mass suburbanization as the only available model for the human habitat.

More than 25 years later, scholar, real estate developer, and author Christopher Leinberger's influential book *The Option of Urbanism* focused on the current and growing demand for more urban living, the kind in line with the New Urbanism and Smart Growth advocacy movements. The argument made by Leinberger and so many others is that suburban sprawl more than any other pattern of development is heavily subsidized by the American taxpayer and is a financial model that, despite its affordable appearances, will continue to strain us, from the scale of the individual household to that of the federal government. Holding these issues up to the light is urbanist and reform-minded provocateur Charles Marohn, who refers to the suburban development process as a Ponzi scheme, an experiment that can be sustained only by the constant growth of still more suburbia.

Despite the huge advancements made by the New Urbanist and Smart Growth movements and their many allies, the most recent national real estate boom, which culminated in the Great Recession of 2007, reflected the same old low-density pattern of development. In these contexts Tactical Urbanism will play an increasingly important role through the type of mobile and temporary services and amenities we describe throughout this book.

Today we are confronted with the legacy of the suburban model and the helpful tools to make urban and suburban areas more livable and sustainable, including Smart Growth, Leadership in Energy and Environmental Design for Neighborhood Development, New Urbanism, low-impact development, smart codes, and sprawl repair.

Of course, not all suburbs are created equal, and these tools are by no means comprehensive. One trend is apparent: The suburbs of tomorrow will be different from today's, for no other reason than the kids who grew up there in the 1980s and 1990s are a lot less interested in returning.

As interesting as the ongoing shift in suburban and urban demographics is, it is perhaps more remarkable that it's occurring despite the vast number of government policies that make this shift more difficult than it needs to be. The growing mismatch between outdated government policy and the demand for infrastructure and urban amenities is a big driver for the rise of Tactical Urbanism. It couldn't have been timed better because, as we'll discuss in the next section, the Great Recession forced almost everyone to do more with less.

The Great Recession and the New Economy

The new century brought a level of wealth and prosperity to the rich in the United States that had never been seen before. For the rest it was merely an illusion. The spectacular burst of the 2007 real estate bubble and the subsequent Great Recession reduced the average American family's wealth to levels not seen since 1989.[7] The idea of inexhaustible growth and an ever-increasing tax base to fund new public facilities and infrastructure quickly went by the wayside. It also revealed that walkable, higher-density places were preferable to their auto-centric, low-density counterparts.

In the words of Tony Schwartz, the "'more, bigger, faster' ethos of the market economies since the Industrial Revolution, is grounded in a mythical and misguided assumption—that our resources are infinite."[8] One need only compare state and local government budgets and services before and after the Great Recession to see how misguided the prevailing paradigm has been. In the first decade of the twenty-first century, municipal expenditures grew by $100 million a year until the start of the recession in 2007. This surge in expenditures was due in no small part to the rapid expansion of municipal services necessitated by suburban sprawl. According to Tommy Pacello, a project manager with the mayor's Innovation Delivery Team in Memphis, Tennessee, between 1970 and 2010 his city's land area grew 55 percent while the population increased only 4 percent. We're not economists, but this is not an economically sustainable approach for any metropolitan region.

Home prices in walkable areas held more value during the Great Recession than their auto-centric counterparts and saw a faster increase in value over suburban areas in 2012.[9] In her 2013 book *The End of the Suburbs*, Leigh Gallagher shows that real estate values are now rising rapidly in places where driving is not the only way to get around. Gallagher explains that from Seattle to Columbus, Denver to New York, the valuation of property in core urban neighborhoods has increased dramatically as housing preferences continue to shift toward compact, walkable neighborhoods. Places such as Seattle's Capitol Hill and Columbus's Short North neighborhood, which for decades were priced lower than newer, fringe developments, now exceed their suburban counterparts, a trend that seems to be accelerating.[10] Indeed, in the 12-month period between 2010 and 2011, housing growth in the core of most North American cities exceeded that of its suburbs for the first time since the 1920s.[11] Smart developers are taking note, as formerly large-scale suburban builders such as Toll Brothers open urban development practices, which in some markets have become their most robust. So what explains this sudden inversion?

The answer lies partially in the diminishing economic rationality of seeking cheap homes built on cheap land at the suburban fringe. This "drive until you qualify" mentality worked to a point for many Americans, but it

Outlying suburbs were hit harder than urban centers during the Great Recession.
(Copyright Alex S. MacLean / Landslides Aerial Photography)

no longer makes sense as transportation costs often match or even exceed housing costs. Proving this point is a 2012 joint report issued by the Center for Neighborhood Technology and the Center for Housing Policy that found housing and transportation costs rose 1.75 percent faster than income in the 2000s, which further strained already stretched budgets. The findings held true for each of the twenty-five largest US metropolitan areas, although the disparity was greater in some areas than others.

Alan Berube and Elizabeth Kneebone, both Brookings Institute fellows and coauthors of *Confronting Suburban Poverty in America*, have found that American poverty, long associated with highly rural and urban areas, has shifted to the suburbs.[12] Census data collected between 2000 and 2011 show that the number of people living below the poverty line in cities increased by 29 percent while in the suburbs it increased by 64 percent. And at present, more impoverished people live in the suburbs (16.4 million) than in core US cities (13.4 million).[13] In *The Great Inversion* Alan Ehrenhalt explains that the inversion of wealth from the suburbs to the city is starting to reflect the spatial distribution of European cities where higher concentrations of low-income people live on the city's outskirts.

This is a positive economic reversal for many American cities' tax rolls, but it also portends a variety of new challenges for metropolitan regions as a whole. The movement of people with fewer resources to housing beyond city centers means that employment opportunities, social services, and low-cost transportation options are less accessible and may further increase the widening gap between rich and poor. With half of a family's budget now going toward housing and transportation, the hidden costs of sprawl are becoming more apparent. Addressing the affordable housing crisis in our most desirable metropolitan areas, such as New York or San Francisco, will require a regional approach to housing, the kind that seems very difficult to achieve.

Regardless of why values held steady or rose in urban places, housing and transportation together consumed an average of 48 percent of the median household's income by decade's end.[14] It is for this reason and others that Millennials and other groups are opting out of the 40-minute commute and choosing neighborhoods that offer not only low-cost transportation options, such as biking and taking the bus, but land use patterns that put more amenities within walking distance. This concept is what the Center for Neighborhood Technology calls *total affordability*, and it almost always favors urban areas, despite the higher home prices. If moving to a walkable neighborhood helps households achieve total affordability, what's the answer for cities?

Since the onset of the Great Recession, municipal budgets have stagnated (or dwindled) while the demand for services, resources, infrastructure, and transportation has grown. As a result, local governments have been forced to rethink the conventional budget process and in many cases to implement a variety of cost-saving measures including hiring and pay freezes, pay cuts, layoffs, furloughs, early retirement incentives, and buyouts. This downshift strained staff resources, which led to delayed or canceled projects and cuts to municipal services and infrastructure repairs.[15] Yet just because tax revenues are not growing does not decrease the pressure on city governments to produce better results, and more cheaply; in fact, it increases those pressures. During times of economic recession, state and municipal governments are more heavily relied on as providers of social safety net services.[16]

The confluence of these factors made conditions ripe for the rise of Tactical Urbanism, at least as it applied to neighborhood-scale projects where citizens took matters into their own hands and governments were forced to adjust their activities with lower-cost and more nimble project delivery methods. In the words of researchers Karen Thoreson and James H. Svara, "Local governments have had to rethink their approaches to doing the people's business."[17]

Luckily, as we'll discuss next, the Great Recession coincided with the ongoing acceleration of existing web- and mobile-based applications calibrated specifically for civic purposes.

Hacking the City

Culture hack. Life hack. Ikea hack. If you haven't noticed, the term *hack* is now being applied to almost any creative pursuit that addresses the perceived shortcomings of contemporary life. However, the term originates from the university computer culture of the late 1960s and 1970s. As one of the early observers (and participants) of the movement, Robert Stallman says computer hackers "typically had little respect for the silly rules that administrators like to impose, so they looked for ways around."[18] Today, hacking is not about an end goal but about the way in which something is accomplished; it's about finding ways around conventional rules to get to an end result, often through an open source and a largely decentralized structure or method. We could not find a better description for the do-it-yourself spirit of Tactical Urbanism. Tactical Urbanism is a way for citizens *and* municipalities to hack the city.

As we described in chapter 2, the idea of hacking as it relates to city planning has been stewing for decades and is found in the work of pioneers such as Bonnie Ora Sherk in San Francisco in the 1970s. For us, the connection between these ideas and the term *Tactical Urbanism* was first made in a post by landscape architect Brian Davis on the *faslanyc* blog, describing New York City's "Greenlight for Broadway" project. Davis referred to the quick changes provided along Broadway as "inexpensive hacks, tactical interventions producing great effects."[19] This description crystalized the idea that Tactical Urbanism owed a large part of its inspiration to hacking culture and the greater infiltration of digital technology in modern life.

In his book *The End of Big: How the Internet Makes David the New Goliath*, Nicco Mele explains the impact, both positive and negative, that digital tools are having on some of our largest cultural institutions. He terms the widespread adoption of handheld digital technology and access to the Internet "radical connectivity." According to Mele, Big Government, Big Education, and Big Journalism have all been disrupted and forever altered by the democratizing effect of access to information networks. And thanks to a wide array of software, hardware, and web-based applications, people no longer need to rely on these once venerable institutions.

The End of Big thesis is highly relevant to the shift we see occurring in the field of urban planning, one where demographic shifts, such as the Great Inversion, are combining with radical connectivity to alter the efficacy and role of one of Big Government's central functions: Big Planning.

"Radical connectivity is about a transfer of power from institutions to individuals. If you asked someone in the early 70s what a computer was, what came to mind was a device that could fill a big room or office. Today 130 million Americans carry around smartphones with the same or greater computing power than a computer from 1974 had," said Mele.[20]

The End of Big thesis is highly relevant to the shift we see occurring in the field of urban planning, one where demographic shifts, such as the Great Inversion, are combining with radical connectivity to alter the efficacy and role of one of Big Government's central functions: Big Planning.

The same changes happening to Big Government have also been happening slowly in the workplace. In a 2012 survey by the employment nonprofit Catalyst, 80 percent of employees confirmed that their companies had flexible working arrangements that included telecommuting and working fewer hours per week.[21] Almost 37 percent of Millennials prefer a flexible schedule over a fixed one. Considering the coming labor imbalance as more

Baby Boomers retire, it's not hard to see how the Millennials (30 percent of the workforce today, 60 percent in 2050) will set the trend.[22]

Although the conventional office building has value, technology has allowed people to work from anywhere, making the city at large a usable office space. The break from corporate office parks and the conventional 9-to-5 model has driven the demand for urban living higher because those locations are the ones with the best existing infrastructure for a flexible schedule (easy access to the Internet and amenities).

In many ways, this is really just an extension of Richard Florida's "street-level culture," which teems with a "blend of cafes, sidewalk musicians, and small galleries and bistros, where it is hard to draw the line between participant and observer, or between creativity and its creators."[23] Urbanization along with the decentralization of the workplace has placed people back in the sphere of street-level culture and in so doing has created a feedback mechanism that will continue to fuel the interest in urban living.

The advent of the Internet, personal computing, and mobile devices and the exponential growth in computing power over the past 30 years have shaped our expectations with regard to the exchange of information, work, social relationships, and government. A whole generation of Americans has grown up with the dominating presence of the computer in their lives. These so-called digital natives (people born after 1980) now account for 47 percent of the total US population according to 2011 census data, a number that will only get bigger with time.

Many argue that the Great Recession simply hastened a trend that was already well on its way before 2007. Thinkers such as Ray Kurzweil and Everett Rogers have been making predictions for years about how both ideas and technology develop and their impact on the economy. Kurzweil has been at the forefront of predicting how the ever-decreasing price of technology will have profound effects on all facets of civilization; this trend is manifesting itself in the economy by creating efficiencies in systems and project delivery processes and by bringing costs down so low "that many goods and services are becoming nearly free, abundant, and no longer subject to market forces."[24]

The unprecedented availability of information and quick communication has created an expectation that change will occur quickly. The expectation of many digital natives and digital immigrants has been established by the rhythmic, almost seasonal change in software for a variety of software programs, apps, and the devices on which they operate. Does anyone remember Windows 3.0? Our expectation as consumers of these products is that with each new generation, something has been improved, a new functionality added, or an old defect abandoned.

There is an obvious downside to the excessive consumerism that comes with the obsolescence of technology, yet our culture has become more comfortable with change in an iterative but fairly rapid fashion. This is the cultural legacy of Moore's law and the exponential nature of technological innovation. Tactical Urbanism is just one cultural manifestation of this idea in the city. It, too, is iterative.

If the past 50 years of technological innovation and evolution are any indication, the next 50 will be just as revolutionary for the way we live and work in cities. In the words of computer programmer Eric Raymond,

> The hacker culture and its successes pose by example some fundamental questions about human motivation, the organization of work, the future of professionalism, and the shape of the firm—and about how all of these things will change and evolve in the information-rich post-scarcity economies of the 21st century and beyond. . . . This should make what we know about the hacker culture of interest to anyone else who will have to live and work in the future.[25]

The implications for urbanists the world over is that radical connectivity actually thrives within the physical framework of compact urbanism because the city is one of the most complex and basic human technologies. The marriage of the digital economy and the traditional city may come as a surprise to those who predicted the demise of urban culture at the hands of the World Wide Web but not to luminaries such as architecture critic Paul Goldberger. In a prescient speech delivered in 2001 at the University of California–Berkeley, Goldberger discussed "Cities, Place, and Cyberspace":

> And for all that the traditional city might appear to be antithetical to the way we live and the way we build and the way we think today, in a metaphorical sense it is absolutely of this moment, for I think of the city not as opposite to the Internet, but as absolutely like it. In a sense, it is the original Internet, the original hyperlink—since

cities are places in which random connections, rather than linear order, often determines what will happen. Cities aren't linear, even though they exist in real space. Random connections are what make them work, and surprise and a sense of infinite choice is what gives them their power. Maybe that is the most important reason of all that old-fashioned cities aren't obsolete—because their very physical form is itself a series of hyperlinks in real space. Paradoxically it is the theme park that is linear, and the old city that represents the new way.

The convergence of the hardware of daily life and the virtual network of the web is one manifestation of the phenomenon often described as "the Internet of things." Simply put, the Internet of things is the network that occurs when objects exchange information without human input. This technology has helped enhance urban living by increasing access to the sharing economy. A *New York Times* article described the trend this way: "This collaborative rather than capitalistic approach is about shared access rather than private ownership." [26]

For example, 1.7 million people globally are members of car-sharing services, a business that keeps growing and would not be possible if not for the ability of each car to communicate its availability to possible users within a network. The implications for urbanism are clear; a recent survey found that the number of vehicles owned by car-sharing participants decreased by half after they joined the service, with members preferring access instead of the burden of ownership. Without any new transit or bike infrastructure, simply deriving new efficiencies from the existing system can drastically reduce the number of cars on city roads.

Millions of people are using social media sites, redistribution networks, rentals, and cooperatives to share not only cars but also homes, clothes, tools, toys, and other items at low cost or for free. The availability of wireless Internet infrastructure has also helped establish a social and tech-based approach that connects the dots between information, a dispersed citizenry, and the government. According to a 2009 survey conducted by the Public Technology Institute in Washington, DC, 75 percent of local government respondents had adopted "RSS feeds to provide news and updates from the government websites to citizens; Twitter to provide emergency, public safety, and other alerts to the public and media; and Facebook to communicate events and a range of other messages with the public. In addition, almost 60 percent of local government respondents said they use YouTube (or similar services) for the purposes of event and program promotion, and to broaden the audience of viewers beyond the reach of public access television channels."[27]

To put this all in perspective, the array of Internet-based communication tools and services we take for granted today didn't exist when we started our planning and architecture careers less than a decade ago. Thus, the speed at which they've penetrated so many facets of our lives cannot be ignored and as much as anything else is responsible for the growth of Tactical Urbanism.

Although new technology allows government to respond more quickly and efficiently, the use of basic technology in planning and government has emerged slowly, especially as viewed by tech-savvy digital natives who want to respond to challenges both digitally and physically.[28]

Many cities still don't have any functional processes online, which means they might as well not exist at all for a growing number of constituents. Of course, there are also people who don't have or take advantage of regular access to the Internet. This so-called digital divide brings up ongoing equity concerns and questions about access to basic goods and services for those who log on infrequently, if at all.

Although hacker culture is about creatively reshaping our surroundings and short-circuiting existing systems, it is ultimately about disrupting existing processes and ways of accomplishing goals. We hope that one of the biggest casualties of the wider adoption of this hacker culture philosophy, especially through the use of Tactical Urbanism, will be some of the more onerous aspects of Big Planning. Indeed, while many call for larger or smaller government, it seems most in the rising Millennial generation stay more neutral and simply prefer better government.[29]

Proponents of what's sometimes called "civic tech" are attempting to work both outside and within government to address these challenges using the latest digital technology. As John Sotsky from the Knight Foundation has said, "The more people use technology as consumers the more they expect technology to shape their experience as citizens."[30] And thanks to the rise of radical connectivity, the convergence of civic needs and technological possibilities is finally taking off.

What has become known as M-government, or mobile government, can be seen in websites and apps such as SeeClickFix, the Daily Pothole, Shareabouts, or TurboVote—a riff on Turbo Tax—that makes it easy to register to vote. Ioby, a "crowd-resourcing" platform for citizen-led neighborhood projects, has become a favorite tool of Tactical Urbanists because it "gives everyone the ability to organize all kinds of capital—cash, social capital, in kind donations, volunteer time, advocacy—from within the community to serve the community."[31]

Radical connectivity is not pulling us apart, as some once predicted, but bringing us closer together, at least physically. Indeed, mobile phones played a central role in the unfolding revolutions, protests, and political changes in the world, from the election of Barack Obama, to the Occupy Wall Street movement, to the Arab Spring. Twitter, Facebook, and text messages helped share the photos and videos that went viral during the recent revolutions in Egypt and Libya, letting people know about protest locations and times—a consequence not only of the mobile apps used for communication but of the wide availability of low-cost wireless devices. These technologies are fundamentally shifting how people participate and organize themselves, yet they are almost always used in conjunction within the traditional framework of the city. As a result, the world now knows Cairo's Tahrir Square, Istanbul's Taksim Square, and New York City's Zuccotti Park. The rise of the Tactical Urbanism movement, though not violent or established for overt political reasons, also relies on the dual infrastructure of the Internet and the physical framework of the city so that together we may all work to address deficiencies in the relationship between government and the people.[32]

The Challenge of Getting Things Done

As more people move to the city or simply choose to stay there, they demand municipal amenities that are not always available, and the formal processes that should facilitate the change they need are lacking. This is as true in former industrial precincts or traditionally underserved areas as in any place experiencing an influx of new residents. As people try to improve their community, they often first approach their city councilor, the local planning department, or even the mayor's office in an effort to bring an idea to fruition. Often it doesn't take long for them to discover that the formal process that facilitates change is often out of date, cumbersome, and far too time-consuming to make it worth the effort. This results in frustration as people feel they have little to no ability to legally use the system, local or otherwise, to enact positive change in their neighborhoods or beyond.

According to a 2013 Pew Research Center analysis, American trust in elected officials reached an all-time low in 2010, from an 80 percent high back in 1956.[33] The disenchantment with the political system and its lack of responsiveness toward the citizenry goes far beyond the shortcomings of the public planning process. The recent atmosphere of cynicism can be traced to a host of factors that are beyond the scope of this book, from war to bailouts for big industry. The frustration created ripe conditions for movements such as the Tea Party and Occupy Wall Street, which come from opposite ends of the political spectrum yet have more in common than most are willing to admit. In general there seems to be a feeling that no matter the level, government should be more responsive to the everyday challenges of the people it serves.

When viewed in this way, Tactical Urbanism is as much about current trends affecting city planning as it is about the relationship—or responsiveness—of a government to its citizenry. And even though the scarcity caused by the Great Recession promoted the adoption of Web 2.0 technologies by municipal governments, there remains a lingering frustration with the formal procedures and processes of our democracy struggling to respond to public demand.[34]

The new people-focused Times Square described in the preface of this book practically appeared overnight, but it was hardly a new idea. The venerable Regional Plan Association proposed not only a car-free Times Square but also a carless stretch of Broadway between Central Park and Madison Square as early as 1969 in their publication *Urban Design Manhattan*.[35] The project, which endeavored to link several of the city's most iconic public spaces and its famed theater district, was positioned as a strategy to keep the city's central business district vital. Although the idea had merit for reasons we'll discuss in chapter 4, the political complexity of permanently closing dozens of blocks to cars—and the lackluster tools planners had to deliver the project against immediate public dissent—would deter even the boldest politicians. And it did.

Yet the era in which the initial Times Square proposal was made was one of transition for the planning profession. The professionalization of the planning field in postwar America left little room for the involvement by citizens in making their own communities. Citizen-led protests and reform efforts followed suit, paving the way for the establishment of some public process, or at least the illusion thereof; the often well-intentioned or regulated inclusion of "the public" today often leaves out wide segments of the population. And although this varies greatly from place to place and project to project, the real challenges facing contemporary city dwellers today is that the process does not serve their interests and or cultural expectations.

Most would agree that municipal government has an important role in regulating land uses and building form. But this often involves separating uses in the way that has taken a serious toll on our transportation network and the social and physical fabric of our communities. And despite widespread knowledge that this regulatory model has outlived its usefulness, municipal governments continue to adopt an overall pattern of development with little public input (in real numbers) or knowledge of how to effectively deliver walkable neighborhoods at a scale that can match the current and coming demand.

The city built in the postwar automobile era never fully developed an effective model for civic engagement beyond regular elections and statutorily required public meetings. And even these methods were weak given the ever-increasing scale of metropolitan regions and their diversity of human and economic capital. As a result, innovative planning processes, those that can be truly inclusive, effective, and efficient in delivering change, have always worked at the margins of an aligned set of disciplines that together participate in an unfortunate professional compact of sorts: Do as much as the budget allows and hope for the best.

The result is an indifference if not disregard for public processes and cultural preferences and a belief that true public consensus may be impossible to achieve. This has played out routinely across the country over the decades. One need only to look at the rise of the historic preservation movement in the mid-1960s *after* the demolition of New York City's old Pennsylvania Station (which was replaced by the current version of Penn Station and Madison Square Garden).[36] Although this event sparked the rise of the New York City Landmarks Preservation Commission and some say the greater field of historic preservation, the real failure was that there was no public process that led to the decision to demolish Penn Station. The *New York Times* reported, "Until the first blow fell, no one was convinced that Penn Station really would be demolished, or that New York would permit this monumental act of vandalism against one of the largest and finest landmarks of its age of Roman elegance."[37]

It was during that same decade that Jane Jacobs's influential *Death and Life of Great American Cities* rebuked the paternal approach to modern city planning. Jacobs's Greenwich Village activism also helped defeat Robert Moses's long-proposed Lower Manhattan Expressway, which would have demolished a large swath of the neighborhoods bordering Canal Street. The struggle to defeat New York City's most powerful leader was a grand and well-publicized display of citizen advocacy. It gave New Yorkers a voice and demonstrated the need to include them in the planning and decision-making process. It also emboldened emergent neighborhood advocates across the United States.[38]

> ... despite widespread knowledge that this regulatory model has outlived its usefulness, municipal governments continue to adopt an overall pattern of development with little public input (in real numbers) or knowledge of how to effectively deliver walkable neighborhoods at a scale that can match the current and coming demand.

The rate at which citizens were seeing their neighborhoods threatened or even destroyed by "urban renewal" did not abate with one defeated highway project. In 1965, Paul Davidoff's seminal essay "Advocacy and Pluralism in Planning" advanced the work of Jacobs and others by critiquing the role planners played in the process of city building. Davidoff believed social justice and equity pursuits were within the purview of planners and advocated for a system that empowered nongovernment organizations and individuals, especially the disenfranchised, through inclusion and public debate. Davidoff relished the type of political tension bottom-up advocacy creates and believed better plans could be achieved by giving voice to the many. "The prospect for future planning is that of a practice which openly invites political and social values to be examined and debated," wrote Davidoff. "Acceptance of this position means rejection of prescriptions for planning which would have the planner act solely as a technician."[39]

But we're still a long way away from effectively including underserved communities in the planning process. Expanding "pluralism" in planning has led to an overly entangled system of federal, state, and local standards, regulations, and process. The process now includes public hearings, written public comment periods, planning and zoning commissions, workshops, charrettes, advisory boards, steering committees, environmental impact studies, permits, and project task forces. Although each has increased levels of public involvement for those with the time and resources to be involved, one has to ask whether the pendulum swung too far in the other direction.

The layers of bureaucracy that must be navigated for projects small and large have become so thick and the process of receiving permission to build so convoluted, given the variety of competing interests and jurisdictions, that it is exceedingly difficult—and expensive—to get anything done efficiently, if

at all. The unintended consequences of this well-intentioned system bloat project timelines and budgets. It also decreases accountability over the years as departmental staffing turns over, economic cycles diminish project scopes (while somehow increasing costs), and plans get redone as politicians' priorities change from one election to another. Our cities are suffering because there is simply too much process and not enough doing.

The destruction of the original Penn Station in 1963 catalyzed the historic preservation movement in the U.S. (Eddie Hausner/The New York Times/Redux)

Examples abound, from San Francisco's much-delayed bus rapid transit line on Van Ness Avenue to New York's Second Avenue Subway to Miami's perpetually delayed Metrorail. We're guessing you can think of at least one similar project in your region. You know the type: large, costly, and complex projects that raise expectations and levels of excitement but ultimately reveal how our current methods of planning pit interests against each other—public versus private, individual versus collective, rich versus poor—rather than seeking to identify commonalities and a smooth way forward. Rome certainly wasn't built in a day, but we're pretty sure it couldn't be built at all today.

Even small projects become wearisome as proponents learn that local government is not oriented to making small-scale change quickly either. There are plenty of people in a given city with the passion and ideas to make small but momentous changes: turning a vacant lot into a dog park, painting intersections with murals, or simply building community rain gardens along their sidewalk planting strip. Yet when it is discovered that implementing such projects takes months of red tape, insurance, and community consensus just to get permission, few have the ability to follow through. The result, in some cases, is that normally law-abiding citizens take action without permission and ask for forgiveness later. It can be a powerful method for creating change.

> Rome certainly wasn't built in a day, but we're pretty sure it couldn't be built at all today.

Just ask Lou Catelli, a resident of Baltimore's Hampden neighborhood, who one evening used spray paint to fashion a crosswalk at a busy four-way intersection. After the city repaved the street in 2011, motorists stopped noticing the stop signs and crossing pedestrians because the city never returned to repaint the crosswalks, stop bars, and street centerlines. Residents and businesses in the neighborhood repeatedly asked the city's public works department to finish the job, but no action was taken because the contractor who repaved the street insisted that cold weather wouldn't allow them to complete the job. Not satisfied with this answer, Catelli took action himself. And during his one-night escapade he reported that the Baltimore police

Lou Catelli, a resident of Baltimore's Hampden neighborhood, used spray paint to fashion a crosswalk at a busy four-way intersection when the City never returned to do the job. (Deborah Patterson)

passed by the intersection three separate times while he was spray painting the crosswalks because of reports of "malicious property destruction." Seeing the civic nature of Catelli's so-called property destruction efforts, the police officers took no action to stop Catelli but reportedly told him to finish the project instead.

Soon thereafter, a spokesperson for the Department of Transportation responded to the "guerrilla crosswalk" by explaining that residents are not allowed to paint Baltimore's streets because of liability issues and that they would investigate if civil or criminal action should be taken against Catelli's efforts. Baltimore city councilwoman Mary Pat Clarke, who represents the area, took a different stance. She responded by saying that the city should be thanking people like Catelli because the visibility and safety of people walking are a priority in the area, especially because of the surrounding schools. Catelli was never charged, and the city returned soon thereafter to complete the striping of the street.[40]

The time and cost required for completing projects, from large infrastructure to small local improvements, is causing citizens and municipal administrators to experience a kind of apathy called planning fatigue. Recovering from this type of civic ennui is difficult, as even the most ardent neighborhood activist or political leader grows tired of the seemingly endless planning process. This explains why the level of frustration with the project delivery system is increasingly tangible among citizens, to say nothing of those paid to administer it. No wonder activists and bureaucrats alike are turning to the immediacy of Tactical Urbanism to hack the system so that they can get *something* done.

RIGHT: Developing more open, transparent, and collaborative project delivery framework should be near the top of any city's planning agenda.

04 OF CITIES AND CITIZENS: FIVE TACTICAL URBANISM STORIES

—

Co-creators fill the ever increasing gap between official action and official resources with their efforts and their presence can be the difference between a city that is "loved" and a city that is merely lived in.

—PETER KAGEYAMA
For the Love of Cities[1]

Children working together to beautify a Portland, OR, intersection. (Greg Raisman)

Behind every successful Tactical Urbanism project there is a compelling genesis story, a tale often born from frustration that leads to a creative response addressing some known challenge in the built environment. In this chapter, we share five such stories elucidating how short-term tactics aimed at disrupting the status quo generated long-term transformation in the physical environment, policy, or both. They are:

- Intersection repair
- Guerrilla wayfinding
- Build a Better Block
- Parkmaking
- Pavement to plazas

In addition, you'll find most contain an additional case study, or a story within a story further contextualizing the impact these initial projects have made elsewhere.

Whether led by enterprising citizens working without permission from city hall or by bureaucrats working from within—government "intrapreneurs"—we want to underscore that small acts do not evolve into larger ones without leadership. Often, the leadership comes from just a small group of people who help bring many, many more people into the process so that they too understand what's possible.

> We want to underscore that small acts do not evolve into larger ones without leadership.

Describing the power and importance of such prioneers, who often go underappreciated by formal community leadership, *For the Love of Cities* author Peter Kageyama writes, "The city, as a whole, is made by a relatively small number of 'co-creators,' who—in their roles as entrepreneurs, activists, artists, performers, students, organizers and otherwise 'concerned citizens'—create the experiences that most of us consume." Kageyama continues, "Many of these co-creators act without authority or centralized direction, and it is from their creative efforts that the rest of us benefit. They make the experiences that we delight in, and they have a disproportionate impact in the making of the city."[2]

Tactical Urbanists are your community's co-creators, and they often blur the lines between city planning, public art, design, architecture, advocacy, policy, and technology. To this last point, each of the stories included in this chapter benefited tremendously from the rise of *radical connectivity*, which we described in chapter 3. For example, Matt Tomsaulo's initial Walk Raleigh "guerrilla wayfinding" project used a suite of web-based tools to create the project, document the installation, advocate for its legitimacy, and ultimately raise the needed funds to get scalability. Or in New York City, Global Positioning System (GPS) units placed in New York City taxis collected and transmitted data allowing the Department of Transportation (DOT) to analyze and substantiate the positive impacts the pedestrianization of Times Square was having on travel speeds through perpetually congested midtown Manhattan.

Today, there are an uncounted number of citizen-led, do-it-yourself, and "creative placemaking" projects being carried out globally by so-called everyday people. However, it's important to note that most of the actors featured in this chapter had some familiarity with the local civic process or received an education background related to the art of city building. This undoubtedly helped make their projects successful. However, we are excited that an increasing number of cities are looking toward the use of Tactical Urbanism as a means to empower nonexperts, those with a lot less familiarity with the conventional project delivery process, to get involved with placemaking. It's a positive trend and one that we think should accelerate.

We hope the projects and the people behind them inspire you as much as they've inspired us to integrate Tactical Urbanism into our professional consulting and personal advocacy work. We attempt to describe the lessons learned from each project throughout the chapter, but we also offer a more complete how-to in chapter 5, which is designed to help you undertake a Tactical Urbanism project in your community today.

INTERSECTION REPAIR

What is the city but for the people?

—WILLIAM SHAKESPEARE
Coriolanus

Project Name: City Repair
Year Initiated: 1997
City of Origin: Portland, Oregon
Leaders: Citizens, enabled by municipalities
Purpose: To develop neighborhood street intersections as community space for increased safety and health
Fact: In the Sunnyside Piazza neighborhood of Portland, 86 percent of respondents living within two blocks of the repaired intersection reported excellent or very good general health, compared with 70 percent in the adjacent neighborhood control site.[3]

Portland, Oregon is a city where a bike path floats on water, lush rain gardens adorn walkable streets, and a delightful array of food carts mask the downtown's few remaining surface parking lots. Although Portland's exceptionalism—real and imagined—has required strong political leadership, it's more accurately a reflection of a progressive citizenry that has developed a culture of civic involvement geared toward transforming the city. Perhaps nothing reflects this better than the story of City Repair and its signature project: intersection repair.

City Repair is an approach to community building and neighborhood placemaking that uses permaculture, natural building techniques, and public art to instigate civic participation. These efforts include intersection repair, which reclaims a neighborhood intersection to make it more attractive and safe enough to serve as a place for neighbors to gather. In Portland, it began with neighbors painting a large mural in an intersection and adding a variety of public amenities such as benches, public information kiosks, and a lending library along the street edges. Intersection repair projects may include private property as well as the public rights-of-way.

City Repair is also the name of the volunteer organization that began

Mark Lakeman's backyard T-Hows created a community gathering place in Portland, OR in the mid-1990s. (Photo by Melody Saunders)

as a loosely affiliated group of activists in 1997. Today, it is a not-for-profit that provides support and guidance for Portlanders and inspiration for those globally interested in improving their neighborhoods through peer-to-peer collaboration. The organization also spearheads Portland's annual Earth Day celebration and has developed an annual placemaking event called the Village Building Convergence, which involves hundreds of people working simultaneously at dozens of project sites across the city.

The organization provides technical assistance for citizens and local organizations interested in developing their own projects. The approach allows communities to take ownership and emphasizes the importance of neighbors creating change together. The organization's leaders are adamant about their role as facilitators, not designers. Such an approach builds social capital and empowers residents because they are directly involved in the funding, design, implementation, and maintenance of the project.

The ascent of the organization and its creation of the intersection repair tactic are instructive because they demonstrate how small, unsanctioned, and low-cost citizen-led initiatives can evolve into much larger city-sanctioned and globally recognized efforts.

When the City of Portland determined that the T-Hows violated the city's zoning laws, Mark Lakeman reassembled it on a pickup truck to create a mobile teahouse, the T-Horse. (Photo by Sarah Gilbert, cafemama.com)

Modeling a Different Future

The City Repair story begins in Portland's Sellwood neighborhood. Located on the southern edge of the city, up on a Willamette River bluff, the neighborhood was then, as it is now, full of modest one- and two-story cottages and bungalows. It was this neighborhood where Mark Lakeman says he began to "model a different future and empower others to achieve it."[4]

Lakeman is the son of a two socially minded architects who taught him the value of planning and design. Lakeman recalls thinking that planners "were like super heroes, envisioning things before they ever existed. It was powerful stuff."[5] Although he later realized how politically charged—and successful—his father's downtown projects were, he also learned that everyday citizens did not play a role in conceiving or building them. Moreover, with their focus on downtown, they did not bring needed amenities to the neighborhoods where most Portlanders live.

After spending several years living abroad and studying the ways other cultures arranged their social and physical living patterns, Lakeman returned home in 1995 only to experience culture shock. Fresh off a stint living and working with Mayans in the Mexican and Guatemalan rain forest, he grew frustrated with how isolated he and his Portland neighbors were from each other, despite living in such close proximity. According to Lakeman, "I looked around and went, 'Nobody here has ever made the choice to zone their life!'"[6]

In an effort to bridge this gap he convinced a few friends to help him create a place where people could meet each other, share resources, and generally build a stronger sense of community. Using natural and recycled materials costing a mere $65,[7] Lakeman designed a small community building where people could meet over tea. He called it the T-Hows (pronounced "teahouse"). It was assembled in the backyard of a Sellwood home and quickly became the site of weekly meetings and potlucks where neighborhood residents met and shared in the amenity of the new community space. It became clear almost instantly that Lakeman tapped into an unmet demand for social gathering space.

Yet the structure was built without a city permit and large enough that it violated the city's zoning laws. After 6 months of growing popularity, city officials finally called for its removal. Always a step ahead, Lakeman had designed the structure to be easily dismantled. He simply reattached the T-Hows materials (recycled Plexiglas, wood, plastic sheathing, and bamboo) to an old Toyota pickup truck to create a mobile teahouse, dubbed the T-Horse. This mobile version was designed to deliver an instant community meeting place wherever it stopped. According to the Social Environmental Architects art exhibit blog, the T-Horse "emerged to transcend the remote power of the city to decide the destiny of communities."[8]

Daniel Lerch, who now works for the Post-Carbon Institute, says that it was while attending an early gathering at the T-Horse with about 200 others that he realized that urban sustainability begins not with light rail systems and LEED buildings but with social relationships. Lakeman's T-Horse, which could be considered a more civic-minded precursor to the rise of the food truck craze, was an intentionally low-cost, mobile, and tactical way to activate public space while also helping people build social relationships across the city.

The T-Horse brought the power of the T-Hows to a much wider audience and quickly became a physical platform for an array of community discussions about strengthening the local economy, placemaking, community empowerment, and environmental sustainability. In discussing the power of creative but simple interventions like the T-Horse, Lakeman states that people "start to see their whole world differently. It's a powerful impetus for change."[9]

With the T-Horse galloping around town, Lakeman moved to reengage his Sellwood neighbors to recreate the magic of the original T-Hows. According to Lakeman, the decision was to transform one intersection into a truly public space, one that would slow traffic and allow neighbors to recreate the intersection as a neighborhood square. The small group chose the intersection of Southeast 9th and Sherrett Streets. As Lakeman said in an interview, "the momentum that we'd built suddenly leapt into the intersection."[10]

Intersection Repair

In the summer of 1996, the group approached the Portland Bureau of Transportation (PBOT) with a proposal to paint the intersection. Because there wasn't a precedent for this in the City of Portland or elsewhere, and despite their lobbying efforts, the group received no support. In fact, one PBOT official infamously quipped in a meeting with the group, "That's public space—so no one can use it!"[11] Inspired by the absurdity of the statement, the group of neighbors decided to move forward a little more creatively.

To subvert the city's stubbornness, Lakeman and his neighbors decided to apply for a standard block party permit to close the streets entering the intersection to cars. However, rather than barbecue and play Frisbee in the street, the group moved forward with a well-considered act of civil disobedience by painting a large mural encompassing the entire intersection. They also built a 24-hour self-serve tea station, a community bulletin board, an information kiosk, and a children's playhouse, which still exist today. From that point forward, the intersection of Southeast 9th and Sherrett was known as "Share-It Square," and Portland's first intersection repair was on view for the city to see.

Not surprisingly, PBOT officials quickly threatened to hand out fines for altering city streets without their permission. The group responded by engaging PBOT and city council members directly, explaining that the project accomplished the goal of slowing drivers and bringing the community together. They were able to back up their claims through a survey they

Share-It Square in Portland, OR. (City Repair)

distributed to neighbors living near the intersection repair project. Results revealed that 85 percent of respondents perceived increases in neighborhood communication and safety and a decrease in crime and traffic speeds.[12]

City council member Charlie Hales understood the project's value and was able to convince the mayor, Vera Katz, and her fellow city councilors that the newly dubbed Share-It Square should not be dismissed for two reasons. First, the City of Portland was experiencing a decrease in funding for art and public spaces, and this group of enterprising citizens had stepped up to address a problem using volunteer labor and donated materials rather than taxpayer dollars. Second, the project was nothing if not consistent with the city's expanding livability policies and sustainability goals seeking more community interaction, less car dependency, and safer streets. So why not let passionate citizens help the city move policy to practice? Heck, why not enable them to do it again in the future?

With Hales's support and 3 months of municipal effort, the city council allowed Share-It Square to stay in place. Moreover, the city began the slow process of crafting an ordinance with simple criteria so that similar projects could be undertaken citywide. Almost 15 years later Charlie Hales (who is currently serving as mayor) told the Sightline Institute about the benefits associated with intersection repair: "It sounds whimsical, but then you go walk around [the intersection] on a Saturday afternoon and you get it. Neighbors are talking, people drive slower, and you can tell you are in a *place*."[13]

Over the next few years Share-It Square continued to evolve: The 24-hour tea station was rebuilt with permanent materials (steel, wood, concrete, and mosaic tiles), the bulletin board was expanded through the addition of a Plexiglas roof and chalkboards, a produce-sharing station opened, and a sidewalk chalk dispenser appeared. Amenities such as benches, neighborhood news kiosks, and other structures have also been added over time, and the original intersection mural has been redesigned and repainted multiple times.[14]

Intersection repair is now defined by City Repair as "the citizen-led conversion of an urban street intersection into a public square." According to Daniel Lerch, who served as City Repair's co-director from 2001 to 2005, the most visible intersection repair element may indeed be the paint, but it's the structures built along the street edge that reactivate the neighborhood because they "introduce a variety of small-scale functions to an otherwise single-use residential zone."[15] In a 2011 article, professor Jan Semenza concurred, "It's not about the paint. It's about neighbors creating something bigger than themselves."[16]

Although it took a few years to wend its way through the municipal process, the City of Portland adopted an intersection repair ordinance in 2000. This meant neighborhoods all over Portland were able to legally replicate the process, and the 3-year-old, all-volunteer City Repair organization was ready and willing to help.

Today, the annual Village Building Convergence involves hundreds of people deploying tactics like intersection repair to make neighborhood improvements across Portland. In a 2012 article about the annual Village Building Convergence, *The Oregonian* interviewed City Repair board member Eddie Hooker about the event's growth. "Three years ago, I ordered 82 gallons of paint for this event. This year, I ordered 267," which were applied to thirty-one project sites.[17] With a stated mission of touching all ninety-six of the city's neighborhoods, City Repair's work, like intersection repair, can now be found throughout Portland.

Not surprisingly, City Repair's work has inspired similar projects in towns and cities across North America, including Olympia, Washington; Asheville, North Carolina; Binghamton, New York; St. Paul, Minnesota; State College, Pennsylvania; and many others.[18] The project's growth in Portland and nationwide proves its appeal and scalability: Neighborhood streets everywhere can be used for far more than just driving and storing automobiles.

Beyond intersection repair, Earth Day, and the Village Building Convergence, the City Repair organization has also spawned several other Portland placemaking and environmental initiatives. Daniel Lerch says this is because City Repair "gives people permission to do activism." Put differently, the people who get involved with City Repair learn the ropes of place-based activism and then shift their focus to other specific areas of need. One example is Depave, which began in 2006 as a loose group of citizen activists removing asphalt—*without* city permission—from underused parking lots and driveways. The goal was to improve the built and natural environments by replacing unnecessary pavement and concrete with community green spaces that mitigate stormwater runoff and the pollution that comes with it.

Thanks to City Repair's trailblazing work a decade earlier and its early role as a fiscal sponsor, Depave quickly transformed itself from an unsanctioned "guerrilla" group into a successful nonprofit organization funded by the US Environmental Protection Agency, the Oregon Department of Environmental Quality, Patagonia, and the Multnomah Soil and Water Conservation Districts. Since becoming a nonprofit organization in 2007, Depave has transformed approximately 110,000 square feet of pavement into expanded schoolyards, community gardens, food forests, and pocket parks. According to the organization's website, the work has resulted in the annual diversion of more than 2,555,000 gallons of stormwater from Portland storm drains.[19]

Intersection repair not only provides a valuable and time-tested Tactical Urbanism example but also shows its power in creating community. Interestingly, the project was undertaken just before the Internet age, yet it has been implemented globally. Information about intersection repair is now widely distributed online, and we believe that it is *the* tactic that helped kick off the most recent wave of citizen-led Tactical Urbanism. Indeed, although its roots are in the mid-1990s, the interest in its use has grown alongside our digital bandwidth, which makes it possible to watch videos, read articles,

and visit websites about why and how the project has been a success. Still, the question remains: Can the social impact of intersection repair be measured?

There is no shortage of claims suggesting that Portland's examples have increased tolerance for diversity, reduced traffic speed, encouraged neighborhood involvement, enhanced neighborhood identity, lowered crime rates, beautified the neighborhood, and offered residents a greater sense of livability. Jan Semenza, a former professor at Portland State University, found many of these claims to be true in a 2003 peer-reviewed article he published in the *American Journal of Public Health*. In the study, Semenza found that Sunnyside Piazza, the second Portland intersection repair project, provided an enriched sense of community. More specifically, 65 percent of nearby residents rated their neighborhood an excellent place to live, compared with 35 percent at a control site (an adjacent neighborhood).[20] Semenza also learned that 86 percent of respondents reported excellent or very good general health, compared with 70 percent in the adjacent neighborhood, and 57 percent versus 40 percent felt "hardly ever depressed." According to Semenza, the success can be attributed to the community-based rituals and process used to create Sunnyside Piazza.

One neighbor interviewed as part of Semenza's research work sums it up best: "It is primarily through the strength and joy of our community involvement that we begin to heal the alienation and disconnectedness so prevalent in American cities."

LEFT: Portland, OR, intersection repair in action. (Greg Raisman)

4.1

Intersection Repair in Hamilton, Ontario

For too long intersections in North America have been designed to maximize motoring at the expense of those not driving. We know this to be a dangerous truth, as Federal Highway Administration data show that in urban areas most fatal crashes occur at intersections.[a] For this reason, we've expanded the definition of intersection repair to include projects where citizens alter not only the pavement surface but also the physical geometry to favor safety for all. The best example we have found of this type of intersection repair is from Hamilton, Ontario, a deindustrializing Lake Belt city of a half-million residents where activists took to the streets to impel sluggish city leaders to move policy and plans to implementation.

Frustrated with the slow pace of change, the Hamilton/Burlington Society of Architects (HBSA) and Ontario Architects Association (OAA) organized in the spring of 2013 to help citizen advocates use Tactical Urbanism to improve the city's catalogue of "incomplete streets." The 2-week effort included a Street Plans–led Tactical Urbanism workshop to develop low-cost and temporary interventions for five intersections representing a range of typical conditions and a 2-week period for participants to implement the projects. To move things along, HBSA member firms put up $5,000 for materials.

With a budget of $1,000 per intersection, the approximately thirty workshop participants—neighborhood residents, business owners, and local architects—needed to be creative. Ideas ranging from guerrilla crosswalks

LEFT: Creating a curb extension in Hamilton, Ontario, under cover of night. (Jeff Tessier)

and wayfinding materials to advancing shared space concepts through theatrical displays of urban design were developed and implemented. The workshop process led to permanent change sanctioned by the City of Hamilton at three of the five intersections, but not without some city–citizen tensions. For this story, we'll focus on the project that drew the most municipal ire but also the most traction.

Herkimer and Locke Streets intersect at the southern end of an old streetcar commercial node on the west side of downtown Hamilton. On the four corners are an auto body shop, an elementary school, a real estate office, and a church. At some point, the east–west running Herkimer Street was converted to a two-lane, one-way traffic pattern, and the curb radii were increased to ease turning for motorists. Despite incessant complaints about safety from the neighborhood and even the completion of a traffic-calming plan, the city had done little to make the street safer for pedestrians.

Workshop participants were asked to identify tactics that could slow cars traveling through the intersection, particularly for the benefit of school-age children, and to get the city to act on its policies. Participants proposed repairing the intersection with "guerrilla bumpouts" so that people walking, especially children, would have less distance to cross and be more visible to motorists, who would be forced to slow down to turn through the junction. The implementation involved three simple steps:

1. Purchase traffic cones, paint them, and then put flowers on top (so there was no way they would be confused with a city-led project).
2. In the dark of night screw the cones into the asphalt to form the bumpout.
3. See what happens.

Traffic calming in action in Hamilton, Ontario. (Philip Toms)

News of the project traveled quickly after an article appeared in the city's leading paper, *The Hamilton Spectator*. Moreover, the local civic issues blog *Raise the Hammer* provided ongoing coverage, including an interview with the school crossing guard, who said, "I like it! It really controls the traffic. It was getting scary."[b]

Despite many similar sentiments, the citizen-led projects were met with sharp resistance from city hall. The cones were removed, and the city manager issued an internal memo alerting his municipal colleagues about the local use of Tactical Urbanism.

These changes to City streets are illegal, potentially unsafe and adding to the City's costs of maintenance and repair. The City can consider this as vandalism, with the potential for serious health and safety consequences for citizens, particularly pedestrians. There is potential liability and risk management claims to both the City and the individuals involved.[c]

Of course, nowhere in the memo did the city recognize the danger of preserving the status quo. Nor did they provide any evidence that the projects brought any harm. Recognizing the irony, public supporters responded with humorous counterarguments in poster form that were spread through social media. In a seemingly orchestrated good cop–bad cop approach, the HBSA stepped forward to claim responsibility and requested a meeting with city officials. Key city councilors and municipal officials agreed and were receptive to the concerns voiced by HBSA, a highly respected local organization. After the meeting, the city abruptly changed its tune. In a brilliant stroke of responsiveness they decided to enhance the Herkimer and Locke Streets intersection, anointing it a "pilot project" to test out higher-visibility crosswalks, curb extensions, and tighter curb radii.

Within 2 weeks of the initial meeting, curb extensions were outlined in paint where the traffic cones once stood, temporary bollards were installed, and high-visibility crosswalks were striped. The response was overwhelmingly positive, which spurred the city to apply similar treatments throughout the city. Checking in on the progress, an August 2013 *Raise the Hammer* article titled "Zebrapalooza" featured an e-mail interview with Martin White, the city's traffic engineering manager. White admitted that the progress was the result of the Locke and Herkimer intervention. Regarding the program's expansion, Martin said the program was initially going to focus on a single neighborhood but proved too popular. "The idea spread quickly and before we could suggest locations, Councilors were coming to us with their higher end requested locations."[d] Within less than a year the City of Hamilton had completed nearly seventy intersection repairs using temporary and low-cost materials as placeholders for a more permanent fix. Within months the city returned to Locke and Herkimer Streets to replace the paint and temporary bollards with concrete.

PHONE THE HAMILTON POLICE SERVICE IMMEDIATELY IF YOU SEE ANY INSTANCES OF TACTICAL URBANISM.

DO NOT TO APPROACH TACTICAL URBANISTS DIRECTLY. PLEASE WAIT FOR THE POLICE TO ARRIVE. THEY MAY BE ARMED AND DANGEROUS, BUT THE TACTICAL URBANISTS ARE UNLIKELY TO BE. FOR ALL SUCCESSFUL ARRESTS, PUBLIC WORKS WILL PROVIDE 10 KG OF FREE ASPHALT.

"Wanted" poster for Tactical Urbanists in Hamilton, Ontario. (Graham Crawford)

Today, the city continues to develop pilot projects and is looking into developing an online platform for citizens to more easily suggest locations in need of improvement by the tools of Tactical Urbanism. HBSA board member Graham McNally writes, "For the City, a Tactical Urbanism program will provide an innovative and effective way to get input from citizens, garner insights and ideas on how to improve neighbourhoods at a scale that is difficult to deal with in Master or Official Plans, and demonstrate to people in Hamilton and beyond that the City is looking to work in new ways and will listen to good ideas whether they come from within City Hall or from outside."[e]

---

a. "The National Intersection Safety Problem," Federal Highway Administration, http://safety.fhwa.dot.gov/intersection/ resources/fhwasa10005/brief_2.cfm.

b. Ryan McGreal, "Invigorating Tactical Urbanism Talk Inspires Action," *Raise the Hammer,* May 8, 2013, https://raisethe hammer.org/article/1849invigorating_tactical_urbanism_talk _inspires_action.

c. http://raisethehammer.org/article/1850/city_crackdown_on _tactical_urbanism.

d. Ryan McGreal, "Zebrapalooza," *Raise the Hammer* August 19, 2013, http://raisethehammer.org/article/1933/zebrapalooza.

e. Graham McNally, "City Embraces Tactical Urbanism," *Raise the Hammer,* September 24, 2013, http://www.raisethehammer.org /article/1960/city_embraces_tactical_urbanism.

GUERRILLA WAYFINDING

Everywhere is within walking distance if you have the time.

—STEPHEN WRIGHT

Project Name: Walk [Your City]
Year Initiated: 2012
City of Origin: Raleigh, North Carolina
Leaders: Initiated by concerned citizen Matt Tomasulo, now walkability advocates, community organizations, and city planners everywhere
Purpose: To encourage walking over other transportation modes
Fact: Although 41 percent of all trips made in the United States are 1 mile or less, fewer than 10 percent of all trips are made by walking or biking.[21]

If the twentieth-century city was about inviting people to drive everywhere for everything, then the city of the twenty-first is about inviting them to walk. In the book *Walkable City*, Jeff Speck says, "Get walkability right and so much of the rest will follow."[22] True. Economic, public health, and environmental gains are correlated to neighborhoods designed to support walking—the kinds of places we've only recently resumed building after taking a 60-year hiatus. As we explore elsewhere in the book, the supply of walkable neighborhoods in America is low, and the demand is becoming increasingly high; one recent study shows that Millennials favor neighborhoods where walking is convenient at a rate of three to one over those where it is not.[23]

Walkability is really just shorthand for everything that creates a neighborhood's desirable character: the quality of architecture, density, humane streets featuring pedestrian-oriented design, mixture of uses, and proximity to parks and usable public space.

But what happens when all these factors are present in a neighborhood but most people living there do not usually walk? How can that culture be changed to embrace travel on two feet? On a cold, rainy night in January 2012, a 29-year-old North Carolina State graduate student named Matt Tomasulo went looking for answers.

In 2007 Tomasulo moved to Raleigh to pursue a dual master's degree in landscape architecture and urban planning. What he found was a fast-growing, highly suburban, auto-dependent city of 425,000 residents. Preferring a neighborhood where driving is optional, Tomasulo chose Cameron Village (Walkscore: 80) because of its proximity to campus and the daily needs that could be reached on foot.

His first experience with Tactical Urbanism was joining fellow students in Raleigh's version of Park(ing) Day, an annual event where citizens around the world pay for a metered parking space not to store a car but to create a temporary, miniature park. Though fleeting, the intervention helps passersby consider a more diverse use of their streets, the need for more public space, and the negative impact auto dependency has on society—or at least those are the stated the goals.

Yet Tomasulo found that his classmates' version of Park(ing) Day did not have the desired impact because it was missing one key element: passersby. "I remember thinking that Park(ing) Day or even parklets don't serve much of a purpose if so few people actually walk by or to them," said Tomasulo.[24] Although he was supportive of the intervention, his own experience with Park(ing) Day and ambling around as a new resident raised a nagging question in his mind: Why do so few people walk? After surveying friends, colleagues, neighbors, and total strangers, Tomasulo says he kept getting the same answer: "It's too far."

He didn't buy it. When we asked about the distances, the normally soft-spoken Tomasulo replied passionately, "It's bullshit! At the time I chose to live between the University and downtown, in a historic neighborhood built for walking, yet so few people would. They would drive two minutes just to get dinner."

So he began mapping the popular destinations people listed when answering questions about where they were headed and how they were going to get there. Was it really too far? He quickly discovered that a majority of respondents were no more than a 15-minute walk from the destinations they named, with many much closer. That's when he realized: The actual distance wasn't the problem, it was the *perception* of that distance.

Although he knew he couldn't permanently change land use, urban design, or infrastructure overnight, he believed he could tackle people's misperception of distance by providing more information. What if the city could display signs with the names of popular local destinations, directional arrows indicating where to walk, and the time it would take the average person to get there? And what if people could scan a QR code on that sign to get directions instantly?

After a little research, he discovered that the City of Raleigh had a number of policies in its comprehensive plan that encouraged walking and were wholly consistent with Tomasulo's intent. However, he also learned that working with the city would be an expensive and arduous process. Indeed, according to Tomasulo, obtaining a temporary encroachment permit for his signs could have taken up to 9 months and would have cost more than $1,000, including the liability insurance costs. The time and money needed were two things Tomasulo did not have.

So he began thinking through how to implement a wayfinding project in line with government policy but carried out without government permission. After researching materials online, he discovered numerous ways to design lightweight and inexpensive "guerrilla wayfinding" signs that would cost him about $300 dollars to produce, or about one fourth the cost of the sanctioned process. He settled on the use of corrugated, weather-resistant Coroplast signs that could be attached to telephone or street lamp poles with zip ties. It didn't take long for Tomasulo to develop a prototype on his laptop. Each sign would inform pedestrians and drivers of the time it would take to walk to popular destinations. He had twenty-seven signs printed and, with the help of his girlfriend (now wife) and a friend visiting from California, went out in the rainy Raleigh night to hang them up. He dubbed the project "Walk Raleigh."

"I knew what I was doing," says Tomasulo. "I very intentionally did not deface public property. I read up on other projects online and realized that we should avoid adhesives; we needed something that could be snipped off easily. This was not supposed to be malicious at all." Pointing to the presence of equally illegal real estate signs found on lawns and telephone poles across the city, Tomasulo says, "They offer no public benefit, yet often remain for months on end. Walk Raleigh at least had a civic purpose and was consistent with the city's stated goals." "I knew that the Comprehensive Plan gave us some justification, wayfinding was already a desired element in the city."[25]

Tomasulo also knew that communicating the project's intent would be important. "I knew the role the Internet could play in expanding the reach of the project." Before posting the signs he bought the domain name walkraleigh.org and created a Walk Raleigh communication platform via a

Facebook page and a Twitter handle. Tomasulo knew the QR codes could help track the number of people interacting with the signs. He also had the presence of mind to document the project with well-composed and high-quality images, which have since been beamed around the world and grace the pages of this book. "We knew it would help us tell a story and hopefully inspire some change. Although, I'll be honest, we didn't really know what would happen next."

Within days the Facebook page received hundreds of "Likes," and the story began to make its way around the urbanist blogosphere, which caught the attention of the *Atlantic Cities* (now *City Lab*) journalist Emily Badger. She included the project, which she dubbed "Guerrilla Wayfinding in Raleigh," as the leading example within a larger Tactical Urbanism project roundup. She noted that "the stunt has actually caught the eye of city officials who may look to make the signs permanent. This is tactical urbanism at its best: a fly-by-night citizen-led escapade whose whimsy could ultimately prompt real improvements to city amenities."[26]

Of course, we've since learned that the "escapade" was not a "stunt" but a well-thought-out and carefully documented intervention intended to inspire long-term behavioral change in citizens and physical modifications from the city. Walk Raleigh was guerrilla. It was also do-it-yourself. But above all, it was *tactical*.

The article in the *Atlantic Cities* brought interest from other national and international media outlets, including the BBC, which produced the story "How to Get America to Walk." The story featured Mitchell Silver, who at the time was serving as the president of the American Planning Association and Raleigh's planning director. Tomasulo, who had never met Silver in person, managed to get Silver involved in the BBC story only after reaching out to him via a direct message on Twitter. Silver responded almost immediately and reportedly rearranged his travel schedule so that he'd be in town to meet with the BBC (Silver later admitted that if Tomasulo had e-mailed him he never would have received or responded to the message in time).

Silver's presence in the story and tacit approval of Tomasulo's technically illegal act made the story even bigger among walkable city advocates. It also demonstrates how, legal or not, well-intentioned citizen-led action often obtains political champions quickly, which then leads to the possibility of long-term change. Silver's proactive response was documented in a follow-up

Matt Tomasulo hanging up Walk [Your City] signs. (Matt Tomasulo)

story written by Emily Badger for the *Atlantic Cities*. "Sometimes something surfaces that forces you to reconsider [ordinances]. This is one instance that we said 'what's going on here?' This wasn't advertising per se. Yes, you need a permit. But we have not seen this level of civic participation in my lifetime."[27]

When news outlets learned that the signs were not sanctioned by the city, they inevitably asked, "Then why are they still up?" This question technically constituted a formal complaint, and the city was obliged to respond by taking the signs down. When they were removed, the citizens of Raleigh protested, asserting that they liked the signs. Sensing the rising disproval of the community, the city moved quickly to figure out how to reinstate the campaign. Silver told Tomasulo that they would make it all happen by making the project a "pilot program" of the city's comprehensive plan. Elated, Tomasulo did his part by rallying community support so that city council would pass the resolution. Turning to the Internet once again, Tomasulo quickly created a signon.org "Restore Walk Raleigh" campaign to demonstrate that there was public support for putting the signs back up.

IT'S A
16 MINUTE
WALK TO
SEABOARD
STATION

IT'S
17 MINUTES
BY FOOT TO
OAKWOOD
CEMETERY

Walk [Your City] signs. (Matt Tomasulo)

Within 3 days the petition solicited 1,255 signatures, facilitated by Tomasulo's burgeoning Facebook following. By the time the city council met, the item was all but foregone conclusion. The city asked whether he'd be willing to donate the signs back to the city for a 3-month, city-sanctioned pilot project. The city officially recognized that the project was consistent with their goals, as stated in their Comprehensive Plan, to increase nonmotorized mobility, enhance bicycle and pedestrian infrastructure, and even expand wayfinding signs.

Spurred by the project's local success and international attention, Tomasulo's graduate school advisor allowed him to change the focus of his master's capstone project so he could focus instead on scaling the Walk Raleigh project initiative. Tomasulo envisioned a web platform where anyone could log on, customize their own signs, and have them shipped within days—zip ties included. However, he would first need some working capital.

To widen the appeal beyond his city, Tomasulo changed the name of the project from Walk Raleigh to Walk [Your City] and turned to Kickstarter, the online crowdfunding platform, to help raise the funds. The Kickstarter staff took a shine to his project and promoted it on their front page, where it garnered more than $11,000 in funding from 549 supporters. This amount was more than twice the initial $5,800 project goal, which was surpassed in just 8 days. "We quickly hit the funding mark, mostly because people were willing to donate $15 without any expectation of a reward," says Tomasulo.

By July 2012 Tomasulo had built a small team and was moving forward with the creation of the Walk [Your City] template, a beta version of which provided editable sign templates for free download. When this began to take off, others were so inspired by the project that they began creating their own "guerrilla wayfinding" projects. Within weeks of the Kickstarter campaign, replicas could be found in New Orleans, Rochester, Memphis, Dallas, and Miami, among other cities.

The downloadable template proved that there was enough demand, and communities began asking Tomasulo and his team to create campaigns to encourage walking. This was enough justification to more fully build out the www.walkyourcity.org platform, which allows anyone to not only customize the digital sign template but also purchase the desired number and have them shipped to a specific location within days. The site's tagline tells visitors, "It's not too far" and provides case studies, instructions and best practices for hanging the signs, and a blog covering projects and the general movement toward walkable cities.

To date, the platform has attracted more than 10,000 sign template downloads and is being used in city and citizen-led projects around the world. Although Tomasulo's efforts took a large amount of energy, vision, and sustained dedication, he claims that it has been worth it. "People in communities as small as 1,500 people to as large as New York City have used the signs. It's low cost and highly scalable. We're proud of that." The platform has even begun to earn some revenue, as local campaigns, advocates, and project managers begin to use the tool and track the data. Back in Raleigh, the North Hills neighborhood has installed ninety-three signs. More than 200 people have scanned the signs for digital walking directions in a period of 9 months. Moreover, Tomasulo says he has been told by visitors and neighbors that although they did not scan the sign, the information on the signs motivated them to take a walk they had never taken before.

Tomasulo's work continues to make an impact in his adopted city. In January 2013, approximately 1 year after Matt hung the signs, the City of

Raleigh voted to adopt a finer-grained comprehensive pedestrian plan, which includes the sanctioned use of Walk Raleigh signs. This unsanctioned to sanctioned project trajectory is consistent with other leading applications of citizen-led Tactical Urbanism projects documented in this book and elsewhere.

There are many lessons to be drawn from the Walk [Your City] case study. Central to all of Tomasulo's work is a suite of low-cost web-based communication and project creation tools exemplifying the power of radical connectivity. As a result, Tomasulo has become a firm believer in accessible, easy-to-use online tools to develop offline action. Tomasulo's work exemplifies what's commonly called civic technology, or "civic tech," which allows people, rather than governments, to effect change.

Tomasulo's work demonstrates how the do-it-yourself approach to civic infrastructure can quickly influence the conventional project delivery process, and it also underscores the point that one can't go it alone forever if the project and its benefits are to be adopted and spread elsewhere in the city.

Moreover, Tomasulo's project demonstrates that successful Tactical Urbanism projects are an exercise in documentation as much as they are in doing. In fact, a key aspect of the Walk Raleigh project is that Tomasulo and his co-conspirators designed more than just physical signs; they researched and designed a process that could increase the chance of success, especially given the initial illegality of the project. The process—research, prototyping, testing, and learning—was deliberate. We'll explore this approach in more detail in chapter 5, but it's worth noting that when the project garnered attention, Tomasulo could clearly articulate why and how he did the project, which helped him forge relationships with city leaders and staff, who quickly learned to see him as a civic leader worth enabling rather than a troublemaker. His web communication platform also allowed him to call on a growing network of supporters when the project was threatened.

So where does the project go next? Will cities across North America begin to use temporary wayfinding signs while the dollars are scraped together for permanent signage? Will the Walk [Your City] effort bring in enough revenue to be sustained for others to use? Does it actually increase walkability in cities? We don't have the answers to all those questions yet, but Blue

RIGHT: Virginia Tech students add their own wayfinding signs to a campus street. (Michael Kulikowski)

Cross Blue Shield of North Carolina is betting that Tomasulo is on to something. In early 2014 the healthcare giant provided Tomasulo with enough funding to hire his first full-time employee, who will help him further guide the implementation of the tool in three different pilot cities across the state. The company views it as a preventive measure against obesity, one that can increase travel on two feet.

While excited about its growing potential, Tomasulo reminds us, "The burgeoning field of civic tech is only a few years old. See.Click.Fix was the forerunner but now there is an explosion of tools and resources available." However, what we do know is that online networks are only becoming richer, and the opportunities to share projects, tools, and ideas for offline action in our communities are growing.

"It is really exciting to see the attitude change, the willingness, and level of support, to take a little more risk, and to team up and troubleshoot how the municipal process can support a project like ours. We just want to build a culture of walking and we think this will help move the needle."

BUILD A BETTER BLOCK

Where bureaucracy, political timidity, or ineptitude all too often prevent places for people, the Better Block just did it, inspired by an outgrowth of frustration with all of the above.[28]

—PATRICK KENNEDY

Project Name: Build a Better Block: Oak Cliff
Year Initiated: 2010
City of Origin: Dallas, Texas
Leaders: Initiated by concerned citizens, scaled nationally by Jason Roberts and Andrew Howard, now used globally
Purpose: To demonstrate all the possibilities for neighborhood transformation in one city block
Fact: The Build a Better Block approach to neighborhood revitalization has been implemented more than 100 times on three continents.

Vacant lots. Empty storefronts. Run-down buildings and rarely used parking lots. Overly wide streets for driving. This is a disheartening scene that can be found in almost every American city. And while many urban neighborhoods are thriving, too many others have not recovered from a half century of systemic disinvestment. Bringing needed amenities to those, young and old, who have endured these conditions is hard to achieve because building rehabilitation costs are high and municipal policies and ordinances remain onerous and outdated. Yet so many of these places have a dynamic social fabric, an interesting history, and possibly a bright future. However, rather than wait for an angel investor or benevolent government agency to play the role of savior, a group of artists and activists in one Dallas neighborhood have shown us that revitalizing our blighted neighborhoods can begin over the course of one weekend.

Because of retail disinvestment and auto-centric zoning, the once bustling Tyler Street in Oak Cliff, a historic streetcar neighborhood located 3 miles southwest of downtown Dallas, embodied many of the characteristics described above. So a small group of neighborhood activists, led by resident Jason Roberts, a musician turned information technology consultant, decided to fix things up. Roberts had cut his teeth on issues of urban planning in successful advocacy efforts that ultimately brought a streetcar back to the neighborhood and helped revitalize the historic Kessler Theatre. However, he felt that the majority of his frustrations were rooted not in individual buildings or modes of transport but in the city's overall approach to land use and transportation. He felt that they were preventing the changes he and his neighbors wanted to see: more bicycle infrastructure, safer streets, and more street life.

"When the streetcar went away in 1956 two of the major streets became one-way, so you lost 50 percent of the [retail] visibility and made it an unsafe, high-speed corridor. These blocks were built *for people*, but the environment around them became inhospitable," asserts Roberts. He brought together a group of like-minded neighbors in 2010 to discuss how to combat the challenges. Roberts says, "We wanted to change the neighborhood, so I got together with fifteen friends, who were mainly artists, in an old theater we helped revitalize a few years prior."

The group discussed the sheer number of barriers citizens must overcome in order to add the placemaking elements that make streets friendly for people. "Why do we still have these ordinances that disallow the congregation of people on a sidewalk? Or require a $1,000 fee just to put flowers on the sidewalk?" questioned Roberts. The city's zoning code also required off-street parking, a pernicious yet common urban policy still found in most American cities that results in more asphalt but also higher redevelopment costs that often stymie would-be small business owners and entrepreneurs. At nearly 70 years old, the Dallas zoning code simply made less sense for how people wanted to live today. No wonder little economic development was happening in this corner of Oak Cliff.

"We were inspired by the work of Shephard Fairey, Banksy and other street artists making people think differently about numerous social issues," says Roberts. "So we began to brainstorm how that line of thinking—the use of highly visible interventions—might be applied to the creation of bike lanes, active storefronts, and other neighborhood amenities we all desired. Collectively, we thought a temporary neighborhood improvement project might help make people think differently about Dallas."[29]

Together the group discussed the common aspects of neighborhood blocks they loved in places like San Francisco, Paris, or even where our office is in DUMBO, Brooklyn. "They all have the same ingredients—a neighborhood hangout, a community market, and active streets. We thought we should try cramming all of these ideas into the street, onto one Dallas block to show people what our neighborhood *could* become." Little did they know that the idea, Build a Better Block (almost called The Perfect Block), would someday help people think differently about moribund blocks not only in Dallas but in cities as diverse as Tehran, Melbourne, and Atlanta.

Using a technique they call "blackmailing yourself," the group publicly announced their intentions in a 2010 Bike-Friendly Oak Cliff blog post penned by Roberts. He described the upcoming project they were now committed to complete like this:

> As part of the Oak Cliff Art Crawl several BFOCers [Bike-Friendly Oak Cliff] along with Go Oak Cliff are creating a "living block" art installation, where we'll be taking a car-centric four lane street with poor zoning and restrictive development ordinances, and convert it into a people-friendly neighborhood block. For two days only, we'll install three pop-up businesses, including a coffee shop, flower store, and kids' art studio and we'll be bringing in historic lighting, outdoor cafe seating, and more. We're working with the set design group, Shag Carpet, and have a team of artists, advocates, and residents all coming together to help pull the project together. Currently, the city creates obstacles for businesses wishing to develop awnings, outdoor seating, live/work spaces, et al. This event is being developed to highlight the changes Dallas should focus on if it truly wants to compete with other major US cities.[30]

Roberts put a strong emphasis on developing a project for and by the neighborhood. "We're trying to dispel the notion this can only be done by architects. Anyone can make a great place, and when you bring this mix of folks beyond just one discipline we'll get great ideas we might not have thought of otherwise."[31]

According to Roberts, the group that assembled to bring the vision to life was a disparate one. "One guy had access to a shop truck, and another one had staging materials, things like historic street lamps and benches. My other friend had a restaurant and we borrowed his coffee urns. Some of my other friends were Etsy artists and we decided they should take over a vacant retail space we had permission to use. My now business partner, Andrew Howard, heard what we were up to and offered help. I didn't know he was an urban planning consultant at the time. I told him to go paint a bike lane. He said he planned and designed them for clients all the time but had never actually made one! He created Dallas's first 'New York–style' parking-protected cycle track."[32]

Howard, who was instantly enthralled with the actual doing involved with the project, called it a living charrette. "There I was, actually painting the bike lanes we normally design on a computer screen. It was a very different and tactile experience. I was hooked."[33]

The effort could be described as not only tactile but tactical as well. The organizing group identified the barriers to revitalization, established a vision for what they wanted their neighborhood to become, and stayed disciplined by starting with just a single urban block.

To facilitate the project the group needed to obtain a run-of-the-mill special event permit from the City of Dallas. Almost every city has such a permit, which is a catchall allowing block parties, art festivals, road races, and other events to occur in the street. The Better Block group organized the event alongside the Oak Cliff Art Crawl, which also requires a special event permit. This made it easier for the group to obtain permission, because as far as the city was concerned, it was just another art festival. However, the "art" in this particular location wasn't on canvases but in the provision of newly created on-street parking, sidewalk dining, sidewalk flowers, parking-protected bike lanes, pop-up shops, and other amenities that were otherwise prohibited or very difficult to achieve. The street also remained open to cars, albeit with an alternate configuration. According to Howard, "We wanted to make it realistic, to show that we could add all of these amenities and the cars could still go through."

True to the spirit of Tactical Urbanism, the Better Block team wanted not just to show what was possible but to show how the amenities created were made illegal by city regulations. So they printed all the ordinances and

RIGHT: Building a Better Block in Atlanta. (Atlanta Regional Commission)

First Build a Better Block, Oak Cliff, Dallas. (Team Better Block)

zoning code roles they were intentionally violating during the event and put them on display for all to see. This form of creative, intelligent, and direct action effectively drew attention to how a 70-year-old municipal zoning code was preventing neighborhood vitality. The conversation this started among city leaders brought almost immediate action to address the outdated ordinances, which alone made the first Better Block project a success.

Impressively, it led to the permanent change that the project organizers desired, perhaps faster than anyone expected. According to Roberts, "Those ordinances we wanted changed were put on the City Council docket for discussion and were changed almost immediately to be more reflective of how we live now. We also got the bike lane we built added to the city's bike plan. And then one of the pop-up businesses—an art shop called Oil and Cotton—leased the empty space they inhabited during the two-day event."

"Instead of town hall meetings, charrettes, and long discussions, just go on-site to where the problem is and start fixing things within days, not years," advises Howard.

The initial Better Block project was such a success that the City of Dallas soon requested the same approach to rapid revitalization to be used in other locations. And with that, Team Better Block was formed under the leadership of Jason Roberts and Andrew Howard. And exactly 1 year after the first

Better Block, the team worked with the City of Dallas's new City Design Studio to help reinvigorate the lifeless City Hall Plaza. In order to understand how such a poorly designed public space could come back to life, Roberts and Howard dusted off famed public space expert William "Holly" Whyte's 1983 plan for the very same space. Although hardly any of the recommendations had been implemented, they discovered that a number of them lent themselves to the kind of temporary entrepreneurial activities and physical design interventions they had used elsewhere in the city.

Armed with this information Roberts and Howard worked with city officials to create the Living Plaza project, which after the first successful demonstration project was made into a monthly event. The city's website says it's designed to "engage city staff in a discussion about urbanism and to demonstrate how great public spaces increase quality of life, improve safety and stimulate the economy."[34] The project also engages the surrounding community, including aspiring entrepreneurs who are invited to test their ideas in the heart of Dallas before they file new business permits and commit to leases.

The City of Dallas should be commended for encouraging this low-cost and low-barrier experimentation, and other cities should consider emulating the approach, which grew from the Build a Better Block method of simply testing ideas in real time.

The Better Block project made an immediate impact locally, but it was a *Houston Chronicle* story[35] and a YouTube video[36] that brought the idea to urbanists across the globe. The first Better Block spinoff occurred only a few months later (October 2010) in nearby Fort Worth. After getting advice from Roberts, advocates in that city sought to improve a mostly vacant and overly wide block of South Main Street. The focus was put on demonstrating a narrower, safer street while also bringing storefront activity to a place where there normally was none.

The City of Fort Worth was not a partner in the original project, yet they were so impressed by the changes that they moved to make some of the project elements permanent. More specifically, the temporary bike lanes that were added to South Main were part of the city's bike plan but had not been implemented because the roadway was under the jurisdiction of the unsympathetic Texas DOT. The Better Block project highlighted the value and opportunity with a temporary bike lane, which inspired the city to obtain the right-of-way back from the state. Two weeks later the temporary bike

Living Plaza project at Dallas City Hall. (Patrick McDonnell/Friends of Living Plaza)

lanes were made permanent. As Roberts says, under normal project delivery processes, "You just don't get bike infrastructure that fast."[37]

The results-oriented Roberts firmly believes that the Better Block technique should be an open source, a tool to aid in neighborhood revitalization everywhere, whether he and Howard are involved or not. This approach has helped inspire more than 100 Better Block projects across the globe, which can be tracked on the Better Block website (www.betterblock.org).

Given the success of many of their efforts, Howard and Roberts, who had begun consulting with cities and organizations across the country, revisited several of their early projects in 2012 and found that most of them led to an almost immediate change in local zoning laws, which is consistent with the results from the team's very first effort in Dallas. Years later, the work of Team Better Block continues to inspire policy change. After working for the first time in Norfolk, Virginia, the city moved quickly to make zoning ordinance changes so that the kind of environment built temporarily could be legalized and made permanent in the future. According to Roberts, "That was literally two weeks later."

There are precursors to Roberts and Howard's Better Blocks from which to draw inspiration. For example, in 1942 the *Atlanta World Daily* reported in an article titled "Better Block Drive Started" that the Atlanta Urban League was initiating a "Better Block" program to "create community consciousness by backing the neighbors and keeping things moving through active partici- pation of the people in the community."[38] The program stressed the impor- tance of local residents sharing common problems and discussing methods to solve them together. A four-block section of the Old Fourth Ward neighbor- hood was targeted for improvement. Garden seeds were handed out to each person in attendance if they pledged to return the next week.

Twenty-six years later, in 1968, New York City partnered with the Bristol- Myers Squibb Corporation to help more than 500 neighborhood advocacy groups participate in Operation Better Block. The director of public relations for the Bristol-Myers company stated, "We had great faith in the premise that the cooperation of private industry, municipal government, and neighbor- hood residents could do a great deal to make this our city, and a better place in which to live and raise our families." The stated goal of the Operation Better Block program was for local residents to "seek, develop, and retain the feeling and sense of 'Community,'" which can be accomplished only through "the creative, imaginative, and joint efforts of the residents themselves."[39]

Inspired by New York, Pittsburgh established its own Operation Better Block program in 1971. The program was designed to help residents in the Homewood neighborhood recover after a particularly long winter that dam- aged landscaping, pavement, and other physical aspects of the community. Residents received seed money to improve the area after residents of each block listed in order of importance what they felt were necessary priorities for the beautification of their blocks. Such priorities included "the planting of shrubbery and trees, individual housing lighting, tot-lots, street lighting, demolition of dilapidated buildings, and regular street cleaning."[40]

Although we don't know much about the results of these early Better Blocks' projects, modern-day projects continue to create permanent change in policy and physical improvements. Harder to measure, but equally if not more important, are the relationships and social networks created during the planning and implementation of the projects. This social capital is developed because so many types of Tactical Urbanism projects require project organiz- ers to ask others for help: The use of vacant buildings or lots, the donation of tools, and the borrowing of materials require one to draw on existing rela- tionships and forge new ones. The economic outcomes of this process can be astonishing. Just ask Memphis, Tennessee.

4.2 Memphis, Tennessee: Inspired to Build a Better Block

In November 2010, just a few months after the initial Build a Better Block project in Dallas, the Broad Avenue Arts Alliance, Livable Memphis, and other community advocates got together in the Binghampton neighborhood to plan a similar but even larger initiative for the moribund Broad Avenue corridor.

Broad Avenue was a forgotten main street that in the mid-2000s began to receive some planning assistance from the City of Memphis in hopes of reviving it. A 2006 charrette brought the neighborhood together and galvanized support for the area's revitalization, but the momentum stopped as the economy went into a tailspin and the city's resources became even more constrained.

A local neighborhood and advocacy group came together to jumpstart their own revitalization effort using the Build a Better Block approach. After speaking with Andrew Howard and Jason Roberts, they raised $25,000 from a group of private and corporate interests for their effort, A New Face for an Old Broad. Pat Brown, a local gallery owner and key figure in the revitalization efforts, and Sarah Newstok of Livable Memphis noted that much of the $25,000 went to pay for establishing access to temporary electricity in the vacant spaces and to pay artists and musicians to be involved in the project (supporting the arts is a big deal in this part of Memphis). The effort included crosswalks painted by students from a local school, six pop-up shops to be occupied by thirteen Memphis businesses, and the implementation of a "road diet" using angled parking and

LEFT: The "A New Face for an Old Broad" event in the Memphis, TN, neighborhood of Binghampton.

Temporary bike lanes and angled parking remained in place after the
A New Face for an Old Broad event in Binghampton. (Mike Lydon)

temporary, parking-protected bike lanes along three
blocks of Broad Avenue.

What transpired next exceeded all expectations.
Using little else but Facebook to promote the event,
they drew more than 15,000 people out for the 2-day
demonstration, which then set off a wave of reinvest-
ment in the Historic Broad Avenue Arts District. As of
this writing the $25,000 A New Face for an Old Broad
event has catalyzed more than $20 million in private
investment for the renovation of twenty-nine properties
and the launching of twenty-five new businesses along
Broad Avenue. It brought the area back into the city's
collective consciousness as a desirable destination.

The temporary bike lanes and angled parking intended
to last for one weekend were never removed, proving the
viability of the more pedestrian- and bike-friendly street
configuration. Later the city began narrowing the street
and adding a cycle track to more formally connect the
neighborhood with the Greenline.

Pat Brown put her finger on it when she told
the *Memphis Daily News*, "It's easier for any of us to

envision what the future can be if you can see it, touch it and taste it as well. Instead of looking at a piece of paper, we want people to experience it."[a]

The project, which connected one of the city's poorer neighborhoods with some of the city's best park space, attracted additional investment and support from the city, local foundations, and the national organization People for Bikes. However, by 2013 a project financing gap of $75,000 remained, so Livable Memphis turned to ioby, a neighborhood "crowd-funding, crowd-resourcing" platform to close the budget gap. Within weeks, the project exceeded its fundraising goal. According to ioby, a majority of the project's donors lived within 4 miles of what is now known as "The Hampline," and the average donation was just $57.

Mayor A. C. Wharton decided to build on the success of A New Face for an Old Broad by directing a 2012 Bloomberg Philanthropies grant earmarked for the creation of the Mayor's Innovation Delivery Team to further apply Tactical Urbanism in revitalizing the city's core neighborhoods. The charge became "Clean it. Activate it. Sustain it." Programs that developed out of this initiative were MEMFix and MEMShop, which used temporary activation, like Build a Better Block events, and pop-up retail tactics to jumpstart the revitalization of neighborhoods.

Memphis mayor A. C. Wharton got it right when he said, "Too often, cities only look to big-budget projects to revitalize a neighborhood. There are simply not enough of those projects to go around. We want to encourage small, low-risk, community-driven improvements all across our city that can add up to larger, long-term change."

We couldn't have said it better ourselves.

---

a. Jonathan Devin, "Broad Ambitions," *Memphis Daily News,* http://www.memphisdailynews.com/editorial/ArticleEmail .aspx?id=54312.

PARKMAKING: POP-UP PARKS, PARKLETS, PARKMOBILES

Project Name: Park(ing) Day
Year Initiated: 2005
City of Origin: San Francisco, California
Leaders: Rebar, citizens, advocacy groups, business improvement districts (BIDs), municipal planning departments
Purpose: To repurpose underused and auto-oriented places into usable public space
Fact: Between 2009 and 2014 the City of San Francisco implemented more than forty individually designed parklets.

With more than 85 percent of the world population living in urban centers, the need is as great as ever to provide access to open space for all city dwellers. Data show that parks and open spaces provide tangible economic, health, and even happiness benefits to residents. One study recently conducted by the Trust for Public Land showed that, among a host of factors, open space on Long Island helped "raise the value of nearby residential properties by $5.18 billion (2009) and increase property tax revenues by $58.2 million a year."[41]

Yet despite the fact that parks and other public spaces have clear health and social benefits for citizens and financial value to cities, many still struggle to provide adequate levels of open space for their residents, especially in low-income neighborhoods. For example, the City of Miami lags behind most US cities of its size in the amount of open space per capita (just 2.8 acres per 1,000 residents, less than a quarter of the 12.4-acre national median).[42] At the same time, parking spaces in urban centers have never been more abundant. One study estimated that there might be more than 2 billion on- and off-street parking spaces in the United States. This is the equivalent of about eight spaces per car![43]

Unfortunately, the type of grand open space plans conceived by the likes of Olmsted in the mid- to late nineteenth century are few, both because municipal budgets are stretched thin and because undeveloped land in urban centers is hard to come by. The tension between increasing need and scarcity of land and resources has created a class of tactical interventions that transform parking spaces and underused road surface into small open spaces serving as public gathering and recreation spaces. Through parklets, parkmobiles,

Philadelphia parklet. (Conrad Erb, www.conraderb.com)

pop-up parks, or pavement to parks (discussed later in the chapter), people around the country are finding new ways of reclaiming space in the public right-of-way and adapting it to fill open space needs.

Parklets provide landscaped and small gathering areas, often in the place of former on-street parking spaces. They serve as an opportunity for a business or organization to try out a park in an area where public space is limited but foot traffic and density are high. Because of their scale and relative low cost, even those that are installed to be used year-round in warmer cities can be viewed as temporary interventions if need be. If the parklet is underused or not well maintained it may be disassembled quickly and inexpensively. At worst, the failure will contribute to best practices data, helping the city avoid underwhelming results in the future, and will be reassembled elsewhere, bringing benefits in a location for which it is better suited.

Parklets range in type and quality, from temporary grass-covered mini-parks to moveable semipermanent wood decks with bike parking, public art, benches, tables, chairs, and even exercise equipment. They are typically characterized by their adjacency to the sidewalk and ability to extend the social life of the sidewalk.[44] Similar to the goals of open streets initiatives, parklets are designed to encourage pedestrian activity and nonmotorized transportation, increase neighborhood interaction and the development of social capital, and increase economic activity in the area.[45] Their purpose is not to replace large city parks but to provide an alternative source of accessible open space in the city that can augment conventional parks. Given the need for open space in dense urban settings, it is no wonder that four of the top cities with low per capita open space (New York, Chicago, San Francisco, and Boston) have been spearheading parklet programs to supplement what are otherwise highly ranked legacy park and open space systems.

The first contemporary parklet, albeit in beta form, is thought to have originated in 2005 with San Francisco–based Rebar, an art and design studio. Yet few know that the Parking Meter Parties of Hamilton, Ontario took place as early as 2001. Local activists there overtook metered spaces and asked fellow citizens to "Bring your musical instruments, gas masks (for the smog), banners, signs, bikes, roller blades, wheelchairs, kitchen sinks, and help de-pave the way to a car free future."[46] It's unclear whether this early work inspired Rebar to create their precursor to the parklet, Park(ing) Day.

Rather than breaking rules and "asking for forgiveness later"–a common practice in Tactical Urbanism–Rebar used another common strategy: They exploited a loophole in the system.

As the story goes, in 2005 two of the leaders of the design firm Rebar in San Francisco went outside around lunchtime, crossed the street, and began installing a minipark in a metered parking space. They set out a bench, added some turf, and dropped in a shade tree. Voilà! A single metered parking space was now a temporary park. When a metermaid asked what they were doing, they pointed out that they had fed the meter and were simply occupying the rented space.[47] "When the meter expired, we rolled up the sod, packed away the bench and the tree, and gave the block a good sweep, and left," said principal Blaine Merker.[48] Rather than breaking rules and "asking for forgiveness later"—a common practice in Tactical Urbanism—Rebar used another common strategy: They exploited a loophole in the system. Nowhere did it say that they *couldn't* use the space as a park as long as they

TOP: The first Park(ing) Day, San Francisco. (Project and image by Rebar Group)

BOTTOM: Noriega Street parklet, San Francisco. (Project and image by Rebar Group)

paid the parking fee. According to principal Blaine Merker, "We researched the code beforehand so we knew that ... we were not breaking the law. We knew that we were operating legally ... exploiting a legal loophole to ... make a point."[49]

This tactical intervention was named Park(ing) Day, and within weeks the initial photo of the intervention traveled across the web. Rebar began fielding dozens of requests to create the Park(ing) Day project in other cities. "Rather than replicate the same installation, we decided to promote the project as an 'open-source' project, and created a how-to manual to empower people to create their own parks without the active participation of Rebar."[50]

The rest, as they say, is history. A few years later the City of San Francisco began to run with the parking-to-park transformations envisioned by Rebar, by working with local business and property owners to launch its now famed parklet program. Although San Francisco has its challenges, the question advocates and urbanists have asked in other, less progressive contexts is how the spirit of Park(ing) Day can be harnessed elsewhere to create long-term change on the scale now seen in San Francisco.

RIGHT: Noriega Street Parklet in San Francisco. (Photo © Wells Campbell Photography)

PUBLIC PARKLET
ALL SEATING IS OPEN TO THE PUBLIC.

4.3 The Rise of Parklets

Park(ing) Day is now an annual event occurring in hundreds of cities around the globe on the third Friday of September, and this modest celebration of Tactical Urbanism has helped spur numerous spinoffs and permanent pilot parklet programs. The City of San Francisco adapted the idea of parklets in its Pavement to Parks program, which reclaimed underused street space and converted it into low-cost public plazas and parks.[a] San Francisco also created the official San Francisco "Pavement to Parks Manual" as a visually pleasing and easy-to-use guide for designing approved parklets in the city. These include the reminder that parklets are public and should feel welcoming to any passersby, whether they are intended for shopping, eating, or patronizing nearby businesses.

San Francisco now has more than forty parklets, with many more proposed and in the permitting process. This program subsequently inspired numerous cities, from Philadelphia to Grand Rapids, Michigan, to develop their own such programs.

In New York City, for example, parklets were first tested when a group of business owners in lower Manhattan sent a letter to the Department of Transportation requesting permission to build public seating in parking spaces near their establishments in parking spaces. None of the businesses were able to build traditional sidewalk café seating because the

LEFT (top): Parkmobile delivery. (Project by CMG Landscape Architecture, image by Julio Duffoo)

LEFT (bottom): Parkmobile in use. (Project and image by CMG Landscape Architecture)

sidewalks were too narrow as defined by the city's guidelines. The city partnered with the businesses and received implementation advice from San Francisco planners who had successfully installed parklets in their city. The first "pop-up café" was installed in 2010 along Pearl Street in Lower Manhattan.[b] A city planner for the Department of Transportation, Edward Janoff, explained that "the parklets fit very well with a message the city is emphasizing: city streets don't need to function the same way all the time. Just because the street is designed with concrete and asphalt, it doesn't need to be used for the same thing. It can be for driving sometimes, and for walking or sitting other times; it can be flexible."[c]

The estimated cost for each permanent parklet varies from city to city but can reach up to $20,000, including permit fees and the cost of replacing meter revenues.[d] Both New York City and Los Angeles provide schematic designs to offset the cost of design that businesses may be unable to afford. As with any sanctioned installation in the right-of-way, parklets require permit applications, design guidelines, community approval steps, and liability insurance provisions that are unique to each city.

A notable offshoot of the parklet is the parkmobile, first proposed in the Yerba Buena Benefit District of San Francisco in 2011. Parkmobiles are made from construction waste dumpsters retrofitted into small green urban oases. Of course, parkmobiles were never intended to handle solid waste but to provide a public amenity across the district. The creative intervention took advantage of a city permit allowing dumpsters to be placed in on-street parking spaces for 6 months before having to be moved elsewhere. This "permit hack" was conceived as a way to bring immediate (and mobile) benefits after completion of a 10-year strategic plan that proponents call "a vision and road map for a next generation of public space in the Yerba Buena District."

The strategic plan included thirty-six projects and was led by CMG Landscape Architecture, which involved neighborhood residents and businesses throughout the district. Other initiatives include widened sidewalks, midblock crossings, and the temporary conversion of alleys into plazas or shared streets.

Given the city's permitting rules, the parkmobiles move around the neighborhood every 6 months, which not only creates a more dynamic streetscape but also brings their benefits (greenery, seating) to different corners of the neighborhood. In doing so, they highlight the importance of an agreeable pedestrian experience and recognize the importance that vegetation and seating play in creating an attractive environment for people. The initiative pays homage to the San Francisco tradition of improving the larger urban landscape in small and fluid ways.[e]

The parklet story shows how quickly good ideas spread from city to city. As the director of the San Francisco Municipal Transportation Authority, Ed Reiskin, said at the time, "I think it helped broaden our thinking when Janette [Sadik-Khan] came and told us what she was doing in New York. There's a spectrum of ways of approaching this right-of-way transformation, some ways such as the plazas and then the parklets could be done a lot faster and easier and can help sow the seeds for future, long-term permanent work."[f]

---

a. UCLA Toolkit, "Reclaiming the Right-of-Way: A Toolkit for Creating and Implementing Parklets," *UCLA Complete Streets Initiative*, September 2012, Luskin School of Public Affairs.

b. Ibid.

c. Ibid.

d. Ibid.

e. "Parkmobiles," Conger Moss Buillard: Landscape Architecture,
   http://www.cmgsite.com/projects/parkmobiles/.

f. Mariko Mura Davidson, "Tactical Urbanism, Public Policy Re-
   form, and 'Innovation Spotting' by Government: From Park(ing)
   Day to San Francisco's Parklet Program," Bachelor's thesis,
   Saint Mary's College of California, 2004, http://dspace.mit.edu
   /bitstream/handle/1721.1/81628/859158960.pdf?se-
   quence=1. Robin Abad Ocubillo, "Experimenting with the
   Margin: Parklets and Plazas as Catalysts in Community and
   Government," Thesis, USC School of Architecture, University of
   Southern California, 2012, http://issuu.com/robin.abad
   /docs/experimentingwiththemargin_abadocubillo2012; Peter
   Cavagnaro, "Q & A: Bonnie Ora Sherk and the Performance of
   Being," Nabeel Hamdi, *Small Change: About the Art of Practice
   and the Limits of Planning in Cities* (London: Earthscan);
   Jeffrey Hou, *Insurgent Public Space: DIY Urbanism and the
   Remaking of Contemporary Cities* (Florence, KY: Routledge,
   2010); *Parklet Impact Study: The Influence of Parklets on
   Pedestrian Traffic, Behavior, and Perception in San Francisco,
   April–August, 2011*, San Francisco Great Streets Project
   (2011), San Francisco, CA.

Bayfront Parkway and the Influence of Park(ing) Day in Miami

Over the last decade parts of downtown Miami have boomed with residential growth, transforming a moribund 9-to-5 environment that hadn't seen growth in 60 years into a vibrant, dense urban neighborhood. The growth has surely benefited the city but has also exposed two fundamental tensions: Usable and accessible open space is scarce, and the surge in development has not benefited many of the neighborhoods that surround the city's immediate core.

One neighborhood where these two issues are most noticeable is Omni/Park West, which abuts the northern edge of downtown Miami. Characterized by vacant lots, surface parking lots held by land speculators, the neighborhood was seemingly skipped over during the development boom. However, because of its transit access and proximity to both Biscayne Bay and downtown, it's only a matter of time before it too experiences the type of investment seen just a few blocks away. However, citizens and local advocates grew tired of waiting and turned to Tactical Urbanism to combat urban blight while satisfying the demand for open space. Each intervention, inspired in part by one that came before, underscored the short-term need to provide more park space to the growing downtown population.

A leader in these efforts was a developer–activist named Brad Knoefler, a retired hedge fund manager from New York. Having lived in Europe for many years before moving to Miami in the late 1990s, he brought his experience of compact, walkable urbanism to the city and spent the better part of the 2000s trying his hand at development by investing in a series of small historic buildings around the City of Miami, including the iconic Coppertone building and the Grand Central building in the Omni/Park West neighborhood.

Knoefler's approach to development did not just stop at the property line. For Knoefler, the neighborhood had to improve hand-in-hand with the building for the development to truly be successful. Indeed, Knoefler is known for deploying a range of creative do-it-yourself tactics to draw attention to blighted properties, including "weed bombing," the act of spray painting overgrown weeds to call attention to neglect.

Another example of Knoefler's civic instinct was his idea to transform the site of the former Miami Arena, which was demolished in 2008. The 5-acre site sits blocks from Biscayne Boulevard and directly across from Knoefler's

The old Miami Arena site. (Brad Knoefler)

apartment in the Grand Central building. As with so many other properties in the neighborhood, the owner had no intention of building in the short term and left mountains of rubble at the site for 2 years after the demolition. Through the rubble, Knoefler saw the potential for the site to become a fairly large and much-needed park.

Knoefler continued working on neighborhood improvements, and in 2011 he partnered with Street Plans to put on Park(ing) Day in Miami directly in front of the site of the old arena. The event was intended to start a conversation citywide, but the chosen location was no coincidence. The event was a big a success, with several hundred residents and local stakeholders attending. The neighborhood's response further catalyzed Knoefler's vision of converting the empty arena site into a park for all to enjoy.

The passionate and tireless Knoefler began researching ways to bring the park to fruition, calling it Grand Central Park. He partnered with LOCAL, a landscape architecture firm in New York that provided pro bono design and planning services to design the park using inexpensive thermoplastic pavement material and a rich palette of native trees and landscaping. In addition to the landscaping, Knoefler and his team also had to figure out how to clear the site of the existing rubble—no easy task.

Knoefler convinced the City of Miami that the project was a good idea and got permission from the landowner to rent the site until the developer chose to move forward with a plan to build. The challenge for Knoefler was to figure out how to derive enough revenue from the pop-up park to cover the hefty lease he committed to paying.

The park lasted 2 years before the property was sold to a new developer, and Grand Central Park was disassembled. However, during the 2 years the park was activated by many very successful and high-profile events that helped Knoefler carry some of the costs. And although the temporary park never became permanent, it did manage to improve conditions in the surrounding neighborhood for several years. And despite being evicted, the

Grand Central Park Group tree planting, Miami. (Local Office Landscape and Urban Design)

remnants of the park remain, a far better placeholder for development than the pile of rubble that existed before.

Grand Central Park wasn't the only lasting impact of Miami's first Park(ing) Day. The city moved forward with its own parklet program, and a local urban planner became inspired to bring the pop-up, temporary park idea to Miami's Biscayne Boulevard.

Three blocks to the east of the temporary Grand Central Park lies Biscayne Boulevard. The grand, palm tree–lined boulevard, constructed in 1926, was transformed into an eight-lane automobile state surface highway over time. The same monuments and palm trees remain, but, sadly, they are now dwarfed by the surrounding parking lots and bloated roadway that cuts downtown Miami off from Biscayne Park, the city's most well-known open space.

Subsequent plans were made to return the corridor to its original grandeur, including the Downtown Development Authority's (DDA) 2009 downtown master plan. However, little was done with the plans until 2011, when local urban planner Ralph Rosado was inspired by the Tactical Urbanism

Grand Central Park, Miami, aerial nighttime image. (Local Office Landscape and Urban Design, photo by Derek Cole)

interventions Park(ing) Day and Grand Central Park. Although he celebrated the idea behind Park(ing) Day, he wanted to use the parklet concept to develop an emergent strategy for realizing a more permanent transformation for Biscayne Boulevard. In his work, Rosado had encountered the DDA's plans to convert the median into a European-style *ramblas*. Thus, Bayfront Parkway was conceived.

Like the plans that came before, the DDA vision was developed under a conventional planning paradigm, one that includes a series of big projects that require securing large but nonexistent amounts of economic and political capital. The plan included transforming the boulevard's 100-foot-wide median parking lots into park space, which would require aligning a wide variety of competing interests and would involve purchasing or leasing the land from the governing body of the parking area, the Miami Parking Authority.

Preliminary estimates placed the earned revenue of the six parking medians, containing 600 parking spaces, at around $7 million a year, to say nothing of the construction of the park, which could run into the millions. Although many elected officials appreciated the vision for the site, few had the political will to sacrifice the $7 million in annual revenue that the parking spaces produced for the city.

Seeking support and co-management of the project, Rosado teamed with Street Plans to implement the Bayfront Parkway vision in a manner that would make an immediate impact and build support for permanent change.

Together, we drafted a plan for a pop-up park demonstration in one of the six median parking lots. They selected a block closest to several new residential towers and raised $10,000 from various entities including the Miami Foundation and the Miami-Dade Cultural Affairs Grant program. The bulk of the money was used to rent the parking spaces from the Miami Parking Authority for 1 week. They used in-kind donations of everything from grass to chairs to umbrellas (everything was donated or returned after the intervention). And arrangements were made with the local fire department to water the grass each morning with the fire truck. All this was done at a fraction of the cost of producing a master plan and having a week-long charrette.

A steering committee was established to guide the project, which included local architects, urban planners, and artists. The steering committee was brought together to divvy up tasks, secure resources, and most of all to build a wider group of people who could use their networks to promote the project but also feel as if they had a stake in the potential success of the park, a smart strategy in building long-term support and political will. The steering committee sought out the work of popular local artist Richard Gamson to design the logo and promotional material for the event and hired photographer Ana Bikic to document the event, from setup to takedown.

Once the hurdle of renting the space was cleared, the committee needed to get approval to host the week-long event in the form of a Special Events Permit, which provides a blanket approval for a variety of activities.

The project team allotted 1 day for installation and 1 day for cleanup, leaving 5 days for programmed open space time. Partners were lining up to participate and offered a variety of programming, from gospel performances, to food trucks, to a drama class held in the park.

The project was hugely successful: The support from thousands of visitors, including hundreds of local residents who knew nothing of the DDA's proposal, signaled it was time to convert the median parking lots permanently. Numerous public officials made appearances at the park to show their support. A common refrain by visitors during the event was, "Is this

Bayfront Parkway before. (Ana Bikic/The Street Plans Collaborative)

permanent?" Letters lamenting the removal of the project poured into the local office of the city commissioner, which was one of several desired results.

The DDA has continued to work on a plan for the corridor since the intervention, developing many options for the closure of the parking lots. Working together with the mayor and other stakeholders, they began negotiations with the Florida DOT for the redesign of the street to include on-street parking, designs for lower speeds, fewer traffic lanes, and improved crossings for people traveling on foot and bicycle. Recently, the DDA took the step of unanimously approving a design concept, which will be the basis for the future design once implementation funding is identified.

Although the project made national headlines as a potential strategy for other cities looking to rethink urban parking lots, its long-term impact remains to be seen. One of the greatest successes of the project was not in the transformation of the boulevard itself but in the shift of one of the partnering organizations: the Miami Foundation. This was the first in a series of public space–oriented grants made by the foundation that led them to establish the Public Space Challenge in 2013. Though not a Tactical Urbanism competition

Bayfront Parkway after. (Ana Bikic/The Street Plans Collaborative)

per se, the contest doles out $200,000 a year to fifteen competitively chosen open space projects that blur the lines between sanctioned and unsanctioned activity. In only 2 years it has helped spawn a dozen creative and inexpensive public space interventions, including a longer-term continuation of one of Bayfront Parkway's more successful elements: a farmers' market.

The story of parklets and parkmaking in Miami is still being written, but the cross-fertilization of ideas is central to the Tactical Urbanism story. As ideas spread from city to city, and then within a city itself, bottom-up citizen-led actions filter up and have the power to fundamentally change the institutions in even the most challenging settings.

PAVEMENT TO PLAZAS

Until a few years ago, our streets looked the same as they did fifty years ago. That's not good business, to not update something in fifty years! We're updating our streets to reflect the way people live now. And we're designing a city for people, not a city for vehicles.[51]

—JANETTE SADIK-KHAN
Former Commissioner of the New York City Department of Transportation

Project Name: New York City Plaza Program
Year Initiated: 2007
City of Origin: New York City
Leaders: New York City DOT, Business Improvement Districts
Purpose: To repurpose underused asphalt space into vibrant, social public spaces
Fact: Between 2007 and 2014, the New York City DOT created fifty -nine new public plazas and repurposed 39 acres of asphalt using temporary materials.[52]

The transformation of Times Square over a weekend in 2009, using folding lawn chairs and orange traffic barrels, introduced this book. You might be wondering how long the temporary transformation lasted beyond the holiday weekend. Maybe you surmised that all of the temporary chairs were stolen; that the resulting congestion, already bad in midtown Manhattan, surely crippled the project; or that a cadre of store owners, cab drivers, and delivery folks joined forces with corporate executives and theater owners to decry the lack of curbside access at the so-called "crossroads of the world." Surely these types of concerns—familiar to some of you, no doubt—and many others would stymie such a novel approach to adding public space in New York City, right?

Wrong.

As of summer 2014, 2 of 5 Broadway blocks are under construction to become permanent public plazas. The remaining three blocks will be

Times Square permanent construction under way. (Mike Lydon)

completed by 2015. These projects are the result of a larger project called Greenlight for Midtown, which converted two lanes of traffic along Broadway, stretching from Central Park to Union Square, into public plazas and traffic-separated bike lanes using temporary materials. Since May 2009, the portions of Broadway through Duffy Square, Times Square, and Herald Square have been closed to automobile traffic, except for crosstown traffic.

Greenlight for Midtown was established to repurpose 200,000 square feet of new public spaces (the size of 3.5 football fields), and was delivered as a 6-month pilot project to be evaluated over the summer and fall of 2009.[53] Movable chairs and tables with umbrellas were placed in all of the plazas, as well as inexpensive but resilient plastic planters full of greenery to be maintained by the local BIDs, including the Times Square Alliance, the 34th Street Partnership, and the Flatiron–23rd Street Partnership. These organizations then began to activate the reclaimed spaces with a variety of social, cultural, and arts programming.

As for the folding lawn chairs in Times Square, they lasted through August 2009 before being recycled into a public art project or given away to

A car-free Herald Square, one of many Greenlight for Midtown public spaces delivered with temporary materials. (Mike Lydon)

those who wanted them as souvenirs. What replaced them were more durable but still inexpensive foldable tables and chairs. Speaking fondly of the intentionally kitschy chairs, Tim Tompkins, president of the Times Square Alliance, remarked, "People voted with their feet and their rear ends and sat down in their chairs. They served admirably and with gusto." [54]

Realizing that the initial interest in the new public spaces in midtown was not likely to be enough to garner broad political and public support for the long term, the New York DOT began measuring the impact of the project's pilot phase. Using crash statistics and taxi-borne GPS units, the DOT discovered not only that Midtown was less congested, with shorter travel times, but that injuries to motorists and passengers decreased 63 percent, and pedestrian injuries dropped 35 percent. [55] They found that foot traffic increased 11 percent in Times Square and 6 percent in Herald Square, which was projected to increase retail sales.

With positive results in hand, mayor Michael Bloomberg announced in 2010 that the project would become permanent, with construction beginning in 2012. Renderings of the more permanent design were developed by the design firm Snøhetta in 2011, while the city and its BID partners continued to measure the project's impacts and increase the amount of programming, even making the Times Square plazas a massive canvas for public art.

By the end of 2013, the cumulative impact of the project revealed that pedestrian traffic had increased 15 percent, to more than 400,000 people per day, while traffic injuries continued to drop and travel times improved. Finally, the ongoing Times Square redesign led to an unprecedented 180 percent increase in area retail rents, making the area for the first time ever one of the ten most valuable commercial destinations in the world.[56]

The Times Square project is the city's most visible example of the city's pavement to plaza program, and its success gave the DOT license to expand the approach citywide. It is being applied at fifty-eight other pedestrian plazas and has been expanded to include temporary curb extensions, medians, and other street design features bringing immediate safety benefits. The visionary leadership and intelligent use of low-cost materials, along with an iterative and flexible implementation process, defined the project and exemplifies how city leaders can effectively use Tactical Urbanism.

At the ribbon-cutting ceremony in December 2013, mere days before she was to leave office, Sadik-Khan proclaimed, "With innovative designs and a little paint, we've shown you can change a street quickly with immediate benefits."[57]

Greenlight for Midtown's success cemented Sadik-Khan's legacy as one of the most inventive city builders in the United States. But the municipality-as-tactician approach in New York City starts with a smaller group of DOT staffers initially tasked with providing safer pedestrian conditions in lower Manhattan in the mid-1990s.

A Brief History of Plaza Improvements in New York City

Societal trends, buttressed by federal policies that subsidized urban decentralization, began to take their toll in US cities after World War II. Urban residents relocating to the suburbs increased the need for Americans to drive. As a result, unsnarling traffic became the singular obsession of not only traffic engineers but planners, politicians, and just about anyone stuck on the road. As in many cities, New York responded by increasing road capacity to accommodate a growing number of automobiles. In tandem with building highways throughout the metro area, New York began narrowing sidewalks and widening streets wherever possible. The city also began replacing the two-way traffic patterns found along Manhattan's avenues with one-way flow, with the idea that these changes would reduce vehicular conflict and delay.

By the early 1960s almost all the avenues received this modern traffic engineering treatment, including parts of Broadway. By 1966 the entire stretch of Broadway south of Columbus Circle was a one-way southbound thoroughfare. Intended to help traffic move through midtown, the modification actually had the opposite effect. Its odd angle and southbound traffic flow delayed traffic each time Broadway crossed another north–south avenue. Nowhere was this more noticeable than at northbound Sixth Avenue in Herald Square. By contrast, Times Square allowed both streams of southbound traffic to proceed simultaneously, with exceedingly long crosswalk pedestrian signals.

At the same time that cities were trying to accommodate more cars on the road, they were redesigning select city streets for pedestrians only to compete with suburban shopping centers. The idea was that bringing the foot traffic and creature comforts of an indoor mall to Main Street would help revitalize districts fast in decline. In their 1977 book *Pedestrians Only*, Roberto Brambilla and Gianni Longo wrote that "pedestrian malls are not urban idylls created in the artist's eye, but practical solutions to some urgent urban problems."[58] Between 1955 and 1980 more than 200 commercial streets were converted to walking-only thoroughfares in American cities large and small. As environmental activism grew throughout the 1960s, pedestrian streets were seen as a way to combat the negative impacts of increased auto dependency as much as flagging retail sales.[59]

As mentioned in chapter 3, the Regional Plan Association envisioned Times Square and the Broadway corridor as a pedestrian street as early as 1969. Unfortunately, the political complexity of closing one of America's densest streets to automobiles at a time when traffic was increasing was not popular. The strategy lacked the necessary tactics and favorable demographic, economic, and social conditions that made the effort a home run 40 years later.

Most of the pedestrian malls implemented at the time were not the savior downtown boosters wanted them to be. In fact, many are blamed for hastening the decline of main street commercial environments and have since been reopened to vehicular traffic (approximately 75 of the 200-plus pedestrian

Paley Park is considered one of New York City's most successful privately owned public spaces. (Aleksandr Zykov)

malls remain today). Yet the factors behind the failure are too often simplified; main streets did not fail because automobiles were deprioritized, they failed because much deeper economic shifts and social trends drove investment, residential populations, and street-level activity elsewhere.

Other programs implemented by the city supported the development of public space elsewhere. Indeed, adoption of the 1961 Zoning Resolution put forth by the New York City Department of Planning offered developers a density bonus in exchange for the addition of public space inside or around their buildings. The program grew to include plazas, arcades, urban plazas, residential plazas, sidewalk widenings, open air concourses, covered pedestrian spaces, block arcades, and sunken plazas.[60] Developers fell in line and so began New York's privately owned public space (POPS) program. Today there are more than 500 POPS areas totaling more than 3.5 million square feet, including Zuccotti Park of Occupy Wall Street fame.

Although the program undoubtedly added public space, quantity did not always equate to quality. Indeed, the shortcomings of the POPS program became a subject of William Whyte's seminal *Social Life of Small Urban*

Spaces (1980), a meticulous inquiry into what constitutes a well-used, safe, and convivial public space.[61] Whyte's work undeniably helped improve privately built and maintained public spaces but did not fully address the challenges of delivering such amenities beyond the city's commercial core or to the increasingly auto-centric streets of America's most walkable and transit-rich city.

Piloting the Pilots

Before the Greenlight for Midtown project, in the late 1990s, New York City began to take smaller, incremental steps to revamp its outdated approach to public space and street design. These smaller experimental projects were invaluable in implementing temporary projects citywide.

At this time Randy Wade, a pedestrian planner with the DOT, was assigned in 1997 to implement the Lower Manhattan Pedestrianization Study. Under normal circumstances, this would include a 10-year process to implement a capital construction project. However, there was strong political will to do it faster and less expensively. With this charge Wade set out to narrow Whitehall Street not with permanent infrastructure but with inexpensive and temporary materials, creating a 2,000-square-foot linear median planting bed using the city's standard jersey barriers. The barriers were painted the color celadon to match the Battery Maritime Building, and consultant Gail E. Wittwer created a small forest of birch and pine. The project team also ordered large but inexpensive plastic planters to further delineate pedestrian space adjacent to new high-visibility crosswalks. They cheekily dubbed the project Whitehall Gardens.

Emboldened by effective use of low-cost materials at Whitehall Gardens, the team took a similar approach to narrowing nearby Coenties Slip, a former inlet used for shipping that was filled in with land and transformed into a street in 1835. The one-block stretch remained wider than most streets in Lower Manhattan and served little to no purpose for automobile traffic. With the goal of reclaiming much of the space for people, Wade ignored the recommendation to protect pedestrians with jersey barriers and found leftover granite blocks from a previous bridge project to designate the new public space. These rectangular blocks were another quick and easy way to protect people from traffic and provided a place for people to sit. Perhaps more importantly for the Downtown Alliance, the BID tasked with maintaining the space, the new "seats" needed almost no maintenance. The Downtown

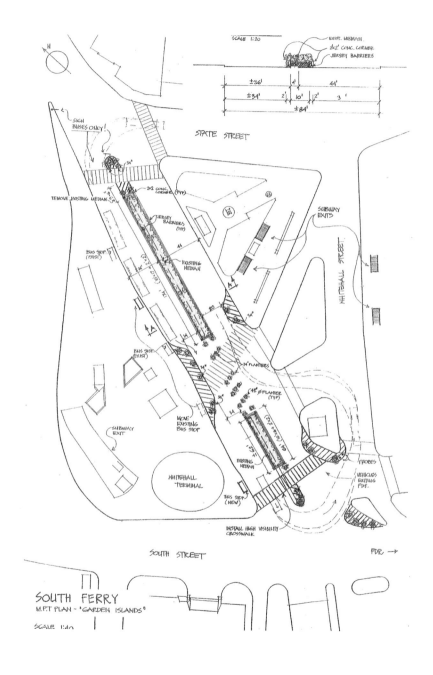

Whitehall Gardens plan. (New York City Department of Transportation)

Coenties Slip today, including recent plaza treatment. (Mike Lydon)

Alliance's Ann Buttenwieser brought in artist James Garvey to hand forge additional street furniture. Completing the pop-up public space project were the same durable but inexpensive planters found on nearby Whitehall Street.

The short-term improvement reclaimed approximately 50 percent of Coenties Slip for people and was an instant hit, especially with the downtown office lunch crowd. The project's success brought a long-term capital investment by the DOT in 2004, which transformed the space further with permanent materials.

Although this pioneering approach to public space development is considered textbook Tactical Urbanism and is standard in New York City today, the temporary-to-permanent approach received little or no attention from those outside the area at the time. Interestingly, the other half of Coenties Slip recently entered the city's current plaza program and at the time of this writing was closed fully to automobile traffic using nothing but temporary bollards, planters, and paint.

After completion of the Coenties Slip project, Randy Wade and her DOT colleagues were called back in 2006 to develop inexpensive off-the-shelf pedestrian improvements in downtown Brooklyn where a little-used street had been identified as an opportunity. By this point, Wade and her colleagues knew what to do. The DOT team partnered with the Metrotech BID to fashion another pedestrian plaza using temporary materials: folding tables and chairs, table and chair units with umbrellas, plastic planters, and whimsical bike racks. They were placed in a low-traffic block on Willoughby Street, wedged between Jay and Adams Streets in downtown Brooklyn. It was here that the idea of pavement to plazas began to be understood as a scalable approach to bringing safety and public space improvements citywide.

Soon thereafter, the idea began to expand more quickly to other areas of the city and was included in the city's landmark PlaNYC sustainability and quality-of-life effort, ushered in by mayor Michael Bloomberg and twenty-five city departments in 2007. After the adoption of PlaNYC, the city took its new pavement-to-plaza program to the northern edge of Manhattan's meatpacking district, on Ninth Avenue between West 13th and 16th Streets, where the DOT reclaimed a wide swath of asphalt at the awkward intersection of 9th Avenue and 14th Street. The project took inspiration from the materiality and aesthetic of the crushed gravel found in the Jardin des Tuileries in Paris. Wade realized the epoxy used to apply no-slip traction to bridges could be repurposed for the asphalt where plaza space was to be created. The result is an attractive, easy to maintain, nonslip environment. According to Wade, "we found the epoxy–gravel mix on the Internet and selected a beige mottled color to create a really attractive, low-cost surface treatment with a cooler temperature to walk on than bare roadbed."

The initial approach Wade's team took to public space enhancement in Lower Manhattan didn't take off at first, according to Wade, because most DOT staff, not to mention fellow New Yorkers, were unaware of the project and its potential scalability. "There wasn't much replication following that first project in 1997," Wade says, "because the treatments were not that visible and they were not connected to a larger political or policy platform." A decade later, the Willoughby Plaza project was hailed as a signal change for newly organized livable streets advocates. These advocates were able to see many of their ideas in PlaNYC. Wade credits the rise of the New York City Streets Renaissance campaign and Streetsblog (founded by Mark Gorton and edited by Aaron Naparstek in 2006), which became the mouthpiece for the whole movement. The city—political leaders, advocates, the business

community—collectively learned that temporary projects are critical because they demonstrate what a street can become. As Wade said, "They are better than a box of paper studies, they let users walk through, sit in, criticize, modify and hopefully love a place to then support the need to make the temporary permanent."[62]

The safety and economic benefits of this pavement-to-plaza program approach are significant, and the DOT devoted resources to capturing and publicizing them in the 2013 report *Measuring the Street: New Metrics for 21st Century Streets.*[63] As in Times Square, the conversion of underused asphalt across the city has led to substantial increases in pedestrian traffic, increases in retail sales for existing businesses, and an impressive decrease in injuries for all street users. Moreover, many of the pavement-to-plazas projects are becoming permanent, including Willoughby Plaza, where the city began permanent construction in 2011 and held a ribbon cutting for the opening in April 2012. Clearly, the short-term and inexpensive improvements are now an accepted if not expected part of the city's street design toolkit.

In a city where every inch of space is of value to someone and therefore contested, framing these types of projects as pilots proved to be a politically deft maneuver. Ardent defenders of the status quo were neutralized by the low cost and temporary nature of the projects. If any of the projects failed from a safety, retail, or quality-of-life perspective, the city said they could revert back to the former condition. Of course, there has been political pushback along the way, but neighborhood outreach and the detailed collection of before-and-after data helped tell the stories of success (many) and failures (a few), which could be accounted for in the next phase of a given project.

Politics aside, the provision of a temporary plaza does not guarantee success for the long term: Removing garbage, folding the chairs and locking them together each night, and activating each space with public art, farmers' markets, music, and other events takes funding and organizational capacity. Thus, a two-pronged management approach that includes regular maintenance and programming has become essential to the pavement-to-plazas program. These responsibilities typically fall on the DOT's maintenance

LEFT (top): Willoughby Plaza before. (New York City Department of Transportation)

LEFT (bottom): Willoughby Plaza after. (New York City Department of Transportation)

partners, which are usually the local BIDs. BIDs form specific geographic boundaries and consist of local businesses that pay tax into a common fund that's used to manage and program the district's public realm.

Of course, not every neighborhood in New York City has a local BID to help manage the plazas, which means the city's program began to leave behind the most underserved neighborhoods that didn't have the resources to maintain their plazas. In 2013, the DOT attempted to address the inequity through an $800,000 public–private partnership with JP Morgan Chase to help economically distressed neighborhoods implement and manage the plaza programs locally. A Streetsblog article covering the announcement quoted former DOT assistant commissioner Andy Wiley-Schwartz saying, "The idea here is to make sure that every neighborhood has the same opportunity. The program was always designed to be citywide, and to work in every neighborhood."[64]

Inspired by the ongoing success of New York's program, several other large American cities have begun to adopt a similar pavement-to-plaza program. San Francisco, which often competes with New York to be the most livable and progressive city in the United States, began a pavement-to-parks program in 2010 and maintains a website (http://pavementtoparks .sfplanning.org/) dedicated to city-led Tactical Urbanism projects happening throughout the city.

After pilot-testing bicycle corrals, parklets, and a single pavement-to-plaza conversion, the Los Angeles DOT launched a new program in 2014 called People St. (http://peoplest.lacity.org/), which packages a variety of off-the-shelf, preapproved materials for reclaiming asphalt in favor of people space. According to Valerie Watson, assistant pedestrian coordinator for the City of Los Angeles, the program is designed to empower citizens, business owners, and neighborhood associations by making the project delivery process faster and more transparent. With People St., the citizens of Los Angeles can now apply to use the city's kit-of-parts (available online) for a range of public space interventions intended to move along the spectrum from temporary to permanent.[65] Each year People St. projects can revert to the previous condition,

LEFT: On Pike/Allen Street in Manhattan's Lower East Side, public space and enhanced bikeways were created using paint and other temporary materials before being upgraded with permanent infrastructure. (Mike Lydon)

apply for a new 1-year permit, or move toward a more permanent project as capital funding becomes available.

Admittedly, trendsetting places such as New York, San Francisco, and Los Angeles are not typical American cities. However, the approach they've developed enabling low-cost and high-impact transformations is needed everywhere and can scale to communities of any size. In fact, for towns and cities with limited resources, the places where Tactical Urbanism projects may be unheard of at the moment, such an approach (temporary, inexpensive, and quick) may be the best and only way forward. Indeed, small towns and cities typically have the least amount of bureaucracy as well. So what are you waiting for? Get started today!

RIGHT (top): Formerly a low-traffic street, New York City's Corona Plaza is now programmed with cultural activities that reflect the rich diversity of the surrounding neighborhood. (Neshi Galindo)

RIGHT (bottom): The creation of Sunset Triangle Plaza gave Los Angeles its first pavement -to-plaza transformation. (Los Angeles Department of Transportation)

4.4   *Pavement to Plazas in Jackson Heights, Queens*

Although New York City residents, business owners, and other stakeholders may advocate for the application of the city's plaza program in their neighborhood, the delivery can still come across as top-down. In contrast, the story of the 78th Street play street turned public plaza in Jackson Heights, Queens demonstrates a successful, iterative, and entirely bottom-up approach to developing neighborhood public space.

Jackson Heights is one of New York City's most vital, diverse, and dense neighborhoods. More than thirty languages are spoken in the neighborhood, and two thirds of the population were born abroad. Despite this diversity, you won't find a lot of variety in the built environment, as the neighborhood has the second least amount of open space in New York. Keenly aware of this shortcoming, neighborhood residents organized themselves into an all-volunteer neighborhood advocacy group called the Green Alliance, which began a play street on summer Sundays in 2008 (see chapter 2 for a historical discussion of New York's play streets program). The play street was located along one block of 78th Street between 34th Avenue and Northern Boulevard, to serve as an extension of the only park in the area, Travers Playground.

The Green Alliance successfully ran the 78th Street play street each summer Sunday for 2 years but wanted to close the street for 2 full months, not just Sundays. However, some residents were worried that the closure would increase loitering and crime at night, decrease available parking, and affect rush-hour traffic. So the

LEFT: Undertaken as a temporary weekend initiative in 2008, the 78th Street Play Street received public-space improvements and is now open to people year-round. (Dudley Stewart)

issue of extending the play street to 2 months was brought before the local Community Board, which initially voted against the idea.[a] Determined to succeed, the Green Alliance organized a 200-person march to a subsequent Community Board meeting in May 2010, where children were among those who spoke about the importance of the play street for their community and health. At the front of the march was Daniel Dromm, a city councilman, who advocated for the extension of the play street. Before the summer of 2010 was in full swing, the Green Alliance had won the local battle to expand the road closure for the entire months of July and August.[b]

The more regular 78th Street play street provided the opportunity for additional programming, which included learn-to-bike clinics, a farmers' market, compost education, organized sports activities, and, of course, the opportunity to socialize with neighbors. According to Dudley Stewart, president of the Jackson Heights Green Alliance, "In the evenings you can have 100 people, people are there well after eight."[c] Though beneficial, all these activities came with a cost, so in 2011 and 2012 residents turned to ioby, the online crowd-resourcing/crowdfunding platform designed specifically to help small neighborhood projects. The group quickly raised $3,402 in 2011 and $2,526 in 2012, which went to programming, maintenance, and sports equipment.[d]

Building from the success of the 2010 and 2011 78th Street play street seasons, the Green Alliance applied to the New York DOT's burgeoning plaza program so that the summer space could be available all year. Although it was a bit of a stretch (the DOT partners mostly with local BIDs), the Green Alliance was chosen as the first all-volunteer neighborhood group to manage a plaza, which would transition the 2-month summer play street into a year-round public space. The more permanent plaza has added approximately 10,000 square feet of open space to the existing playground through the city's capital budget project delivery process. In recalling the group's initial success, neighborhood resident Donovan Finn said, "A lot of what it took was just people seeing it in action. That was the proof."[e]

---

a. Noah Kazis, "Jackson Heights Embraces 78th Street Play Street and Makes It Permanent," Streetsblog NYC, July 5, 2012, http://www.streetsblog.org/2012/07/05/jackson-heights-embraces-78th-street-play-street-makes-it-a-permanent-plaza/.

b. Ibid.

c. Ben Fried, "Eyes on the Street: 78th Street, Jackson Heights, 8:15 PM," Streetsblog NYC, August 6, 2010, http://www.streetsblog.org/2010/08/06/eyes-on-the-street-78th-street-jackson-heights-815-pm/.

d. "Jackson Heights 78th Street Play Street 2012," Ioby.org, https://ioby.org/project-jackson-heights-78th-street-play-street-2012.

e. Kazis, "Jackson Heights Embraces 78th Street Play Street."

05 A TACTICAL URBANISM HOW-TO

—

In order to do something big, to think globally and act globally, one starts with something small and starts where it counts. Practice, then, is about making the ordinary special and the special more widely accessible — expanding the boundaries of understanding and possibility with vision and common sense. It is about building densely interconnected networks, crafting linkages between unlikely partners and organizations, and making plans without the usual preponderance of planning. It is about getting it right for now and at the same time being tactical and strategic about later.

—NABEEL HAMDI

Opportunities to apply Tactical Urbanism are everywhere—from a blank wall, to an overly wide street, to an underused parking lot or vacant property. As we have described, citizens may use Tactical Urbanism as a tool to draw attention to perceived shortcomings in policy and physical design, and municipal authorities, organizations, and project developers may use it as a tool to widen the sphere of public engagement, test aspects of a plan early and often, and expedite implementation so that it's easier to build great places. We describe such initiatives as *tactical* because they use a deliberate and accessible means for achieving preset goals while embedding flexibility into the planning and project delivery process. Using the framework of design thinking, in this chapter we'll explain our approach to any Tactical Urbanism project, drawing out specific lessons for citizen or government tacticians wherever possible.

Design Thinking

The professionalization of the hacking movement has brought with it a number of techniques and processes for responding to new or persistent challenges. One such method is "design thinking," which is not so much a noun as a verb. The basis for design thinking developed in the 1960s, but its contemporary application was developed at the Stanford Design School and the consulting firm IDEO under the leadership of brothers Tom and David Kelley. In the book *Creative Confidence*, the brothers Kelley define the process as combining empathy for the context of a problem, creativity in the generation of insights and solutions, and rationality in analyzing and fitting various solutions to the problem context.[1] In recent years its popularity has risen alongside the growth of technology start-ups, many of which have adopted its core tenets along with many of the product development methods prescribed in *The Lean Startup*, by Eric Ries.[2]

Design thinking is not a completely foreign concept to the allied disciplines of city building. Peter Rowe, a Harvard professor of architecture and urban design, adapted the idea to the field in the 1987 book *Design Thinking*. However, the concepts presented in Rowe's book did not penetrate the field. But as technology firms and start-ups have gained cultural cachet over the last two decades, more attention has been paid to how the application of contemporary design thinking does and does not translate to city building. In our experience the five-step design thinking process is valuable for producing successful Tactical Urbanism projects. Both design thinking and Tactical Urbanism recognize that design, like city building, is a never-ending process where absolute solutions are rarely if ever achieved. The steps are similar to the problem-identification-to-project-response process commonly used by Tactical Urbanists. The five steps are:

1. Empathize: Understand for whom you are really planning or designing.
2. Define: Identify a specific opportunity site and clearly articulate the root causes of the problems that need to be addressed.
3. Ideate: Research and develop ways to address the defined problem.
4. Prototype: Plan a project response that can be carried out quickly and without great expense.
5. Test: Use the build–measure–learn process to test the project and gather feedback.

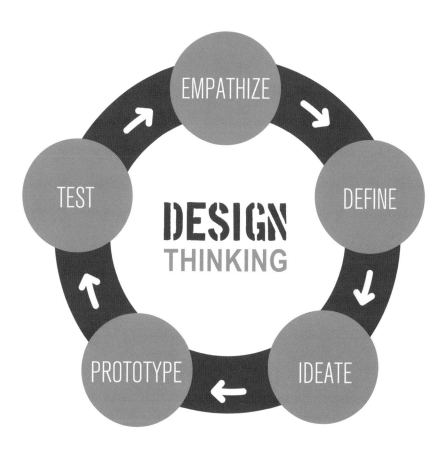

Design thinking. (The Streets Plan Collaborative)

These steps do not need to be followed in a linear fashion, they often overlap, and they should be repeated as needed. The steps should be considered a framework for addressing a variety of urban problems writ large. The how-to process described in the pages ahead provides details for how you can apply it to your work.

1. EMPATHIZE: UNDERSTAND FOR WHOM YOU ARE PLANNING OR DESIGNING

All Tactical Urbanism projects seek to address a deficiency in the built environment. However, an effective project response cannot be developed until you understand for whom you are really working.

Often, you are working for you, but also friends, family, or unwitting neighbors. Individually or collectively, you grow tired of a rundown building, an unused parking lot, or an overly wide street, so you take action, with or without permission. Although this can be effective, it's important to consider who else may be affected by your project so that you can take their needs into account as well. How would your older neighbor down the street, the shop owner on the corner, or the child next door respond? First, we advocate asking them; even if you are not seeking to address their needs specifically, it's important that your project not make things worse for them. If you receive feedback about the potential of negative impacts, you can make adjustments. On the other side of the coin, you'll probably find you're not the only one who has been adversely affected by an undesirable element in your neighborhood. Taking a shot at making things better will also attract like-minded people who have often thought to undertake a similar project.

For those working in a professional capacity, a client, a local politician, or a department leader may determine some or almost all aspects of a project in advance. If this is the case, get out of the office immediately and head to where people are in the project area. You can gain firsthand knowledge by asking well-considered questions of citizens. This will help you ground truth your ideas with stakeholders and possibly identify others who should be considered as such, including those who do not often participate in the conventional planning and project delivery process.

Developing this basic level of empathy is probably common sense for many readers, but just take a walk in most towns or cities and you'll quickly understand that those planning, designing, and regulating our built environment often fail to understand hyperlocal issues and the diverse needs of the people their work purportedly serves.

For example, many traffic engineers do not put themselves in the shoes of the most vulnerable roadway users, those who navigate the end result of their engineering and design work with something other than a speeding 2-ton automobile. This lack of empathy for others means we often get convenient environments for some at the expense of safety for all, including those driving. To combat this problem, safe streets advocates have begun to take city leaders, planners, engineers, and public works officials out of their cars and into the streets to actually walk, bike, or use a wheelchair in the deadly environments they produce. This simple exercise costs no money and can begin

The 16th Street bike lane, Miami Beach, demonstrates a lack of empathy in planning. (Mike Lydon)

to produce a very different type of result as the ignorant become educated through one of the most powerful communication and empathy-building tools: personal experience.

2. DEFINE: IDENTIFY A SPECIFIC OPPORTUNITY SITE AND DEFINE THE ROOT CAUSES OF THE PROBLEMS THAT NEED TO BE ADDRESSED

Tactical Urbanism is not a silver bullet. It won't solve many of the pressing challenges we find in our towns and cities, but it can respond to and raise awareness about persistent problems found throughout our neighborhoods.

Places that are ripe for a Tactical Urbanism intervention are what we call opportunity sites. In some instances, the site is so clearly underperforming—economically, socially, physically, or environmentally—that it becomes a clear target for an intervention. These locations often make themselves known through feedback loops such as previous community planning efforts, mounting citizen complaints, crash data, or crime statistics. However, not every opportunity site is obvious, nor can all these sites be addressed at once. Indeed, many of the most persistent problems remain unchanged for decades despite the many plans that have called for their transformation. So with all the possibilities, how do you choose a good one?

SITE SELECTION: AT WHAT SCALE?

Scale and physical context matter tremendously in the site selection process. When we have a choice, we like to apply Tactical Urbanism to places that feature base conditions that exist elsewhere. If it is successful, the chance that the project response could be adopted elsewhere or formally adopted into municipal planning and policy is increased. But whether it is conceived as a neighborhood project in itself or as part of a larger planning effort, we recommend shrinking the scale and narrowing the scope of your intervention wherever possible. This can be difficult for many of us who want to jump to a more comprehensive vision for change. But stay disciplined; think about issues across the neighborhood but act at the scale of the building lot or street corner. You can always scale up your efforts later, and we hope you do. Or, if you must, focus on matching the scale and context of your site with an appropriately scaled tactic. Getting this right will often lead to the next project opportunity, phase, or location.

As mentioned earlier, chair bombing is the act of addressing our nearly universal public seating deficit by placing chairs or benches where they do not yet exist. It's one of the more simple and effective tactics. But doing this on a lonely sidewalk in front of a suburban strip mall adjacent to a five-lane arterial where few people walk may not be very effective. The space between buildings is simply too diffuse, the speed and volume of traffic too high for comfort, and the number of potential users too low for such a small-scale intervention to make an impact.

Although this scenario is hypothetical, an authentic and well-scaled response to a similar condition is found in the Audubon Park Community Market in Orlando, Florida. Located on Winter Park Road, just steps from the five-lane Corinne Drive, the market occurs every Monday night in a strip mall parking lot serving several local businesses, including a popular café, a salon, and a bike shop. The weekly happening appeals to the adjacent businesses' clientele, who appreciate the local food, music, and crafts sold

RIGHT: Audubon Park Community Market day and night. (Mike Lydon [top] and Michael Lothrop [bottom])

there. The market also competently makes a temporary, well-laid-out, and programmed public space out of what is normally a sun-baked and car-filled parking lot.

Organizing the Community Market certainly takes more time than putting chairs next to the sidewalk (chair bombing), but the payoff is commensurate with the effort. Today, the market's success has served as a low-risk and consistent market study proving demand for a more permanent market space in the neighborhood. As a result, those who began and maintain the weekly effort have recently opened East End Market, a two-story brick and mortar version of the night market, a mere two blocks away. There, visitors will find local food stalls, books, antiques, office space, and a small community farm located out front. This effective temporary-to-permanent response demonstrates the importance of what professor Nabeel Hamdi describes in *The Placemaker's Guide to Community Building* as "scaling down to scale up—working backwards to go forwards."

SITE HISTORY RESEARCH

Although not all project sites have a compelling history, researching recent and past buildings, uses, street design configurations, and programming may aid the site selection process by further defining the challenges and opportunities associated with a given site. As with the Times Square, Dallas City Hall, and Bayfront Parkway projects profiled in chapter 4, plans proposed in some form much earlier but never implemented for political or economic reasons may provide insight and inspiration. Thus, we recommend visiting your local library, the municipal archives, or the web to find useful information before fully defining the opportunities at hand.

THE FIVE WHYS

Once the opportunity site is selected and understood both physically and historically, it will be important to define the root cause of the challenges found there. This may occur in a number of ways, but we suggest trying "the Five Whys," a technique developed by Sakichi Toyoda to optimize his company's auto manufacturing process. Toyoda observed that problems in manufacturing are often the result of flawed processes, which can be discovered quickly by simply asking "why?" multiple times (he found five to be ideal). This simple exercise is known to produce important insights, has become a key part of the lean manufacturing process championed globally, and is used by a variety of creative disciplines as well.

We've adopted the Five Whys exercise into many of our Tactical Urbanism workshops because the weaknesses people are so quick to point out in their neighborhoods are typically the physical manifestation of something beyond the perceived problem: a flawed human process, an outdated and forgotten municipal policy, or some other root cause none of us think to address. As it turns out, using a physical intervention to highlight these items can be an easy and cheap way to ensure that the same mistakes are not repeated long into the future, and, ideally, it can inspire a long-overdue policy change.

Take a few minutes and give it a shot. Think of an issue that bothers you in the neighborhood in which you live or work and phrase it as a problem statement. Then, ask yourself why that problem exists. Give it some thought and then answer the question. Once you have your first answer, rephrase it again as a question. Repeat this process as many times as necessary until you feel like you've arrived at one or more of the root causes. This should help focus your intervention so that it addresses the root cause.

The Five Whys technique is not perfect. Indeed, as you practice the technique you'll find that sometimes you'll need to ask the question more often, and sometimes less. You may also arrive at a few competing root causes that will require increased dialogue or the need to test multiple project responses. That being said, we've found that the Five Whys exercise helps us quickly define and prioritize the types of challenges and opportunity sites that need to be addressed first. From there, the fun can begin with a more focused round of brainstorming. This should focus on creating a project response in the short term that is intended to make an impact on policy, process, or physical design in the long term.

3. IDEATE: RESEARCH AND DEVELOP WAYS TO ADDRESS THE DEFINED PROBLEM

Brainstorming project ideas—ideation—is one of the most delightful aspects of the Tactical Urbanism process. All ideas should be considered as long as they use the knowledge gained from step 1 (Empathize) and are focused on addressing the challenges and opportunities defined in step 2 (Define). The ideation process may happen with individuals, small groups, or even large assemblies. For example, Matt Tomasulo developed the Walk Raleigh campaign on his own, the first Build a Better Block was the outgrowth of a small number of dedicated and creative Dallas residents, and the Bayfront Parkway project involved no fewer than thirty Miami organizations.

Each approach has value. For instance, individuals and small groups can often move quickly through the first two steps of the design thinking process and develop internal consensus and use resources efficiently. Larger groups allow project proponents to build broader consensus and tap into greater networks. This can enrich the ideation process and will prove valuable when it's time to source project funding, materials, volunteers, and marketing assistance. That said, developing a wide network is a benefit at any stage: The sooner people get involved with an intervention, the sooner they take ownership of the project. Although the size of the group and ideation methods will vary, the task should always involve figuring out *what* to do and *how* to do it.

> Merely mimicking a successful project is perilous because it's difficult to ascertain the social, economic, political, and physical context in which the project takes place.

WHAT TO DO?

The most basic project ideation technique is to look at the work of others. Thanks to the Internet, researching is easier and faster than ever before. Thus, it's likely that you'll find several blog posts, news articles, and self-made You-Tube videos documenting where creative and scalable approaches were used to tackle common challenges. We certainly do this early and often for all our Tactical Urbanism projects. However, like any search for precedents, it should be one for inspiration and helpful information. Merely mimicking a successful project is perilous because it's difficult to ascertain the social, economic, political, and physical context in which the project takes place. Yet too often this is what we humans do: We seek to mimic success through imitation.

An endless number of creative workshop techniques and idea-gathering tools are available for use in planning projects, beyond setting up flip charts

A simple installation using Neighborland stickers engages passersby in considering what constitutes a Lifelong Community. (Mike Lydon)

and laying out markers on a map. For open public initiatives, the combination of both online and in-person ideation platforms, such as Neighborland (https://www.neighborland.org), are the most effective because they make documenting, sharing, and connecting project ideas in your neighborhood easier and more effective than ever. Neighborland is the outgrowth of artist and urban planner Candy Chang's "I Wish This Was…" project, which began with the playful tweaking of name tag stickers, which were then placed on vacant or blighted buildings so that passersby could share their reuse ideas for post-Katrina New Orleans.

Other tools such as Mindmixer and Crowdbrite can also widen engagement beyond typical public meetings and workshops and allow the easy collection and organization of ideas and public input data. In particular, ease of use and a visually pleasing interface are driving the dramatic increase in the use of online tools. But are they worth it?

It depends on the project and the context (and funding). Merely allowing the public to cast votes or discuss projects online is a certain kind of participation, one that can add value. However, sometimes these tools are used as part of conventional initiatives looking to goose project participation numbers. Eric Ries calls these "vanity metrics."[3] Sure, increased clickthrough participation can make us all feel good. But after the ideation process is completed, a few questions almost always remain: Now what? Are the ideas and projects actionable? Did the online tool actually help facilitate offline collaboration and implementation?

These kinds of questions lead to what Ries calls "actionable metrics," which should be used to provide a clearer path forward. For Tactical Urbanism projects, actionable metrics should be established so that project ideas advance quickly to the prototype and testing phases described in the pages ahead. We turn to Everett Rogers, an early sociology scholar of innovation, to help you consider the "actionability" of your Tactical Urbanism project ideas.

In the seminal text *Diffusion of Innovations* (1962), Rogers identifies five factors that influence whether we humans adopt or reject innovation: relative advantage, compatibility, simplicity, trialability, and observability.[4] Although much of his writing focuses on the spread of technology, each of these factors may be turned into a question during the project ideation phase to help you think through whether your short-term project response will effectively address the problem you've defined and ultimately lead to long-term change.

- *Relative advantage:* Will the project actually provide an advantage over the status quo for an identified group of people?
- *Compatibility:* Is the project compatible with its social and physical context, in both scale and scope?
- *Simplicity:* Can the project be easily understood by a wide segment of the population?
- *Trialability:* Can the project be tested easily? Can it be easily replicated elsewhere? Is the path to adoption clear and relatively hurdle free?
- *Observability:* Is the project going to be visible to many others? Will it attract use and attention?

Asking these questions will benefit your project tremendously.

HOW TO GET STARTED: SANCTIONED VERSUS UNSANCTIONED PROJECTS

There are only two ways to approach a Tactical Urbanism project: with permission or without. And the ideation stage is the perfect time to decide the right path to pursue.

If you have never taken on a project in partnership with the city but are considering it, then it's best to talk to someone with some experience working with local government. So-called municipal tacticians do exist, and their role is to guide enterprising people like you through a multitude of municipal processes or spotlight policy or permitting workarounds that help you deliver the results they know benefit the city but they themselves may struggle to achieve. Unfortunately, municipal tacticians who relish this role are hard to find, because they often work with little fanfare and are conditioned to deflect attention. Again, ask someone with local experience who might give you the right names from the right department. From there you can make a more informed decision about whether to pursue a sanctioned or unsanctioned project approach.

If you are a government employee—self-identifying municipal tactician or not—the answer is usually clear. Overt action carried forward without the backing of municipal process is usually frowned upon, if not grounds for your censure or even dismissal. As you might know all too well, this results in a risk-averse culture at city hall that offers little or no reward for disrupting the status quo. Still, innovative bureaucrats are increasingly finding ways to slash red tape, help project creators find the right loophole, or enable new types of projects through the formulation of new policy (see the story of New York's pavement-to-plazas program in chapter 4).

We generally recommend that project proponents consider a city or organizationally sanctioned approach if two or more of the following conditions are met:

- The project is large in scale and complex in nature. Roughly, this means something that may require the use of city property, more than a few hours to implement, or more than a modest amount of funding.
- Project champions are likely or have already been identified and are willing and able to help proponents obtain or expedite permits (if needed), assist with insurance and liability concerns, help source needed materials, and even provide funding (if you're lucky).
- The proposed project may be tied to a current planning effort or is consistent with existing plans, policies, or project delivery protocols. Creative city and organizational leaders interested in Tactical Urbanism will need the political cover to help justify their assistance with the effort.

Unfortunately, few city governments are set up to enable or deploy Tactical Urbanism projects. As a result, citizen-led action tends to shock the system, which is perhaps best exemplified by the chapter 4 stories of intersection repair we highlighted in Portland, Oregon and Hamilton, Ontario. Yet cities of all sizes stand to benefit from these expressions of civic participation and should realize that small legal infractions are wonderful opportunities to engage in a dialogue with project proponents (and opponents) about how the city can best address their concerns. To be sure, we advise that city leaders focus less on the illegality of temporary interventions of this sort and more on the underlying conditions that cause constituents to act without city permission in the first place. When cities do this and treat their citizenry as co-creators, not as scofflaws or vandals, the response is usually met with tremendous respect and support from the discerning public.

In this way, the unsanctioned-to-sanctioned examples we shared in chapter 4 (Intersection Repair, Walk Raleigh, Park(ing) Day, Build a Better Block) demonstrate that municipal government can and should work proactively with citizen leaders rather than crack down on their activity. Such projects are highly visible and should be considered a low-cost way to engage a wider audience of people.

Although sanctioned projects often provide legitimacy (and funding) from the beginning, they may take many months if not years to come to fruition. But unsanctioned projects can be completed very quickly because urban tacticians generally hope for the best and rely on exploiting loopholes (like Park[ing] Day) or asking for forgiveness later.

We generally recommend that project proponents consider an unsanctioned approach if two or more of the following conditions are met:

- The intervention is small in scale and easy to pull off.
- All conceivable sanctioned channels have been pursued and municipal leaders seem unwilling to address existing plans, policies, and project delivery protocols with the proposed project.
- No municipal permit or sanctioned process workarounds can be identified.
- A high level of confidence exists that the project will be viewed favorably (or at least with indifference) by abutters, neighbors, and other community members.

Of course, this type of work doesn't come without risk. Just ask Anthony Cardenas, a Vallejo, California resident who was arrested for painting a high-visibility crosswalk (with zebra stripes) across the busy four-lane Sonoma Boulevard. Having witnessed several crashes and nearly becoming a victim of traffic violence himself, Cardenas took matters into his own hands after city engineers ignored his requests. A week later, the paint was traced back to the source and he was arrested. However, an anonymous donor paid the $15,000 bail, and Cardenas was given a hero's welcome upon returning to the neighborhood.[5] One grateful neighbor, an employee of a nearby hair salon, told the local newspaper, "We have a special place in our heart for him because we have a business here, and we're all women, and we get out very late....He will walk us out to our cars and make sure everything's fine.... This is a very bad street."[6]

It should be recognized that even in cases where citizens illegally intervene on public property, the intent is rarely, if ever, malicious. In addition, if unsanctioned projects are to succeed in the long term, they ironically must return to the bureaucratic processes the proponents hoped to avoid in the first place. Thus, in the long run citizen tacticians should expect to work within institutional and political processes to realize permanent change. Likewise, institutions and municipal governments will know project proponents are serious when they are seeking collaboration for the long term.

Although arrests are very rare, they do happen. The case of Anthony Cardenas is one unfortunate example. However, we've still never heard of anyone being seriously hurt or killed as a result of an unsanctioned Tactical Urbanism project. We wish we could say the same about the dangerous, sanctioned status quo conditions so many Tactical Urbanists take on.

4. PROTOTYPE: PLAN A PROJECT RESPONSE QUICKLY AND INEXPENSIVELY

Once a definitive site and project response have emerged—the need to calm traffic, make a bus stop more comfortable, or develop a neighborhood gathering space—it's time to design a lightweight and inexpensive version of the idealized long-term response. Call it an intervention, a prototype, a pilot, whatever. Just make sure you move the idea to action quickly.

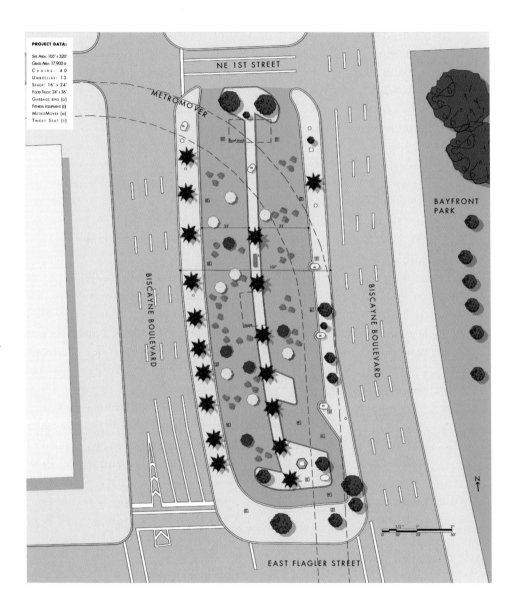

PROJECT DATA:
Site Area: 105' x 320'
Gross Area: 17,900 sf
C h a i r s :   4 0
Umbrellas: 13
Stage: 16' x 24'
Food Truck: 24' x 36'
Garbage Bins (g)
Fitness Equipment (f)
MetroMover (m)
Tweet Seat (t)

NE 1ST STREET

METROMOVER

BISCAYNE BOULEVARD

BISCAYNE BOULEVARD

BAYFRONT PARK

EAST FLAGLER STREET

B A Y F R O N T   P A R K W A Y
MEET ME IN THE MEDIAN!
February 29 - March 4

presented by
Corzo, Castello, Caraballo, Thomson, Salman, PA.

presented by
The Street Plans Collaborative &
TransitMiami.Com

PROJECT PLANNING

Although many Tactical Urbanism projects, sanctioned or not, may appear to be spontaneous, even the lightest intervention requires *some* planning. This includes considering the physical design but also logistical elements such as who (if anyone) will help, when to undertake the project, how the project will be funded, and what materials should be used.

At this stage, it's important to remember that what makes your project tactical is the intent; the short-term intervention should be placed within a framework for delivering long-term change. To do this, we often use a process called 48x48x48, which was developed in 2011 alongside DoTank:Brooklyn for a project we completed in downtown Oyster Bay, New York. In short, the 48x48x48 process intentionally links the immediacy of a 48-hour intervention with two additional and subsequent time scales: 48 weeks (short term) and 48 months (medium term). The "48" is arbitrary, but the point is to accept the limitations of the typical 20-year plan and to build flexibility into shorter feedback loops so that shifting priorities and conditions can be accounted for. It is for this reason that we advocate limiting the Tactical Urbanism project timeline to 4 or 5 years, at least at first. Not only is this time horizon much easier for people to wrap their minds around, it aligns fairly well with 4-year political cycles and 5-year capital budget processes.

IDENTIFY PROJECT PARTNERS

The goal of your Tactical Urbanism project is to create a lasting physical or policy change, so partnerships within the neighborhood and across sectors will be not only beneficial but necessary. We've found that the most successful Tactical Urbanism projects bring together partners with a diverse set of skills. Even if you are initially working alone or in a small group without permission, finding partners to fulfill the following roles will be helpful as you formulate your project.

- *Moneymakers.* In many cases, fundraising is what enables ideas to be moved to action. Fortunately, the rise of easy-to-use crowdfunding platforms has helped project proponents unlock small amounts of capital (often in small individual contributions). Successful

LEFT: The Bayfront Parkway Plan envisioned transforming a parking lot into a large pop-up park. (The Street Plans Collaborative)

Howard Blackson prototypes knock off surveillance signs to discourage trash dumping as part of a "take back the alley" initiative. (Mike Lydon)

crowdfunding initiatives do require project proponents to treat their efforts like a campaign, and it's helpful to have someone develop a compelling title and clear message that may be delivered in a number of digital mediums. If the delivery of your project is not scheduled for the very near future, finding someone with grant seeking and grant writing skills could also be helpful. Additionally, finding people with the chutzpah to go door-to-door and business-to-business is another way to raise funds while simultaneously building community awareness for the project. All of these skills may not be needed for your project all at once, and they probably can't be found in a single person. Therefore, if you don't have such fundraising skills we suggest partnering with a few people who can help get the resources your project needs.

- *Hunter–gatherers.* Identifying the materials you'll need is a different challenge than actually obtaining them. Matching project needs with the right material resources at the right (low) price is a skill unto itself and often requires persistence. If you are not sure what materials are out there or where to look for them, find friends or colleagues who do. They'll be invaluable.

- *Makers (design and construction).* Let's be honest: Not everyone is good with a hammer or a chop saw. Although developing these skills can be useful, soliciting help from family, friends, and other volunteers who possess design and construction skills is recommended for some kinds of projects, particularly for citizen-led projects where city resources are not to be used. Finding collaborators with these skills will make the buildout of the project—no matter how small—that much easier and safer and will build connections for future project endeavors. Hey, you may even get pretty good on that chop saw.

- *Coordinators.* The larger the project, the more likely it is to take the sanctioned route. This can be great, but please know that it also means a greater amount of coordination will be needed. Thus, having two or more leaders who can manage the various project logistics—securing insurance, permits, security, rental equipment, volunteers, site access, and more—may be necessary. Fortunately, an increasing number of project logistic tools are now available. For example, Team Better Block has developed an online volunteer management portal for their projects that wisely breaks individual project components into standalone classes where participants learn skills and build capacity around topics such as developing project metrics, building pallet furniture, and reactivating public spaces.

- *Mouthpieces.* We can't emphasize enough the value of communication in the delivery of a successful Tactical Urbanism project. For the less "secretive" projects, social media and blogs are a good place to share the project and its goals and an absolutely critical tool for building awareness. For unsanctioned projects, you should at least document the installation and final product so that you can get the word out anonymously. That said, it's always helpful to include project partners who have media and marketing contacts and expertise. This will help you explain to the general public why you are doing the project and how they can be involved. Moreover, a clever project name, brand, and message will help the public identify the project and communicate its intent. Indeed, creative titles, bold graphics, and inviting messaging will help spread the word. Examples we like are "A New Face for an Old Broad," "The Parkside Park-In," and "Park(ing) Day."

PROJECT SCHEDULE

Whether sanctioned or not, a project schedule, including both time and date, should be developed once the details of the project emerge from the ideation process. Though not appropriate for all project types, we generally recommend scheduling implementation so that it aligns with and leverages the visibility of already established local events, including art walks, open streets, road races, or similar community-oriented initiatives that draw larger-than-normal crowds. This will increase the project's visibility and help build demand for its longevity.

For sanctioned projects, committing to a project implementation date early and announcing it publicly are important steps for material procurement, permitting, and marketing. They also give you little or no choice but to move forward with the project. Indeed, most people respond much more proactively to truncated timelines and more immediate deadlines than to longer time horizons. As mentioned in chapter 4, Jason Roberts of Team Better Block refers to this technique as "blackmailing yourself."

PROJECT FUNDING

How do you fund Tactical Urbanism projects? As you might imagine, this is one of the most common questions we receive. The answer is short: Any way possible! In all seriousness, Tactical Urbanism projects are made possible through an increasingly wide variety of funding support mechanisms. For many projects, little or no funding is needed as project leaders borrow, reclaim, or have materials donated for their efforts. In these instances, all that is needed is the courage to ask and thank-you notes to send later.

Additionally, some of the more successful projects we've documented have cost a few thousand dollars or less yet have helped leverage millions in new investment, such as the A New Face for an Old Broad project in Memphis (see chapter 4). However, as the movement becomes increasingly mainstream, more standard municipal, foundation, and corporate funding streams are being used to fund creative placemaking and Tactical Urbanism initiatives, including urban prototyping festivals, make-a-thons, and design-and-build competitions. To that end, we recommend that you consider thinking about how your project fits within existing funding guidelines, local and regional policies, ongoing planning efforts, and philanthropic initiatives. Many Tactical Urbanism projects address transportation, health, and environmental initiatives already funded by governments, corporations, and foundations. For example, we already mentioned that the Walk [Your City] initiative has attracted funding from Blue Cross Blue Shield and that the Depave effort in Portland, Oregon is now funded by a variety of government and corporate sources. Remember, both of these initiatives, like so many others, began with absolutely no funding or municipal support. So if you are struggling to get up and running, don't let money be too much of a deterrent. Implementing a successful project with only modest resources is impressive and requires the creativity that often attracts funding *after* your first prototype is made visible to others.

Finally, citizens and organizations are now able to bypass traditional paths of project funding, and the strings attached, by leveraging their social media networks with compelling project pitches. Although hard work is needed, crowdfunding platforms such as Kickstarter have allowed us to tap into an entire market of financial backers for even the quirkiest projects, tactical or otherwise.

Of course, Kickstarter is not the only crowdfunding platform out there today, and industry experts expect crowdfunding to grow from as much as $4 billion in 2014 to nearly $300 billion in the years to come.[7] Other industry leaders include Indiegogo and our favorite Tactical Urbanism fundraising tool: ioby. Ioby refers to itself as a crowd-resourcing platform that helps neighborhood projects come to life block by block. Although most projects funded on ioby are small in scale, it has also helped big projects get over the funding hump. For example, in Memphis ioby was the crowdfunding platform of choice for raising nearly $70,000 to close the funding gap for the Hampline, an on-street protected bikeway that is one of many permanent changes resulting from the A New Face for an Old Broad better block project.

PERMITTING

For many, the municipal permitting process is an anachronism from the pre-Internet age. In most communities the process lacks transparency and has not evolved to facilitate the kind of citizen-led projects that define the

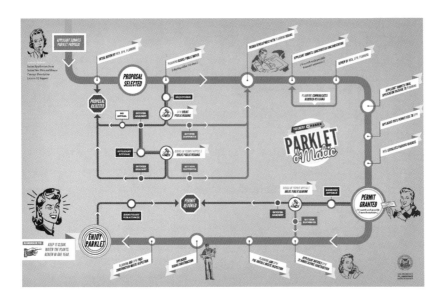

TOP: San Francisco's Parklet permitting flowchart is designed to be more engaging than most city processes. (City of San Francisco)

Tactical Urbanism movement. However, if you're taking the sanctioned path, you'll need to get permits for most project types.

For buildings, a temporary use or occupancy permit will often allow you to activate vacant or underused indoor space, provided you have permission from the property owner. The restrictiveness of such permits varies from city to city but should allow you to avoid bringing spaces up to the most current building, fire, and disability access codes—an expensive and onerous process. From the beginning of your discussions with property owners you'll want to work out the issue of insurance. Some property owners may be fully supportive and allow you to come in under their policy. In other cases, a project sponsor (e.g., a city or organization) may name the property owner as an additional insured, keeping their liability to a minimum.

For public space (e.g., sidewalks, streets, parks), you'll probably be directed to apply for a special event or large gathering permit to facilitate your project. These serve as catchalls for a wide variety of events such as block parties, concerts, outdoor art fairs, and road races. Once your site is selected you'll want to take note of all of the entities with jurisdiction over different aspects of the street. This could include the city, county, regional transit authorities, departments of transportation, parks, local utilities, and others who may need to sign off on various aspects of the project.

You can also expect that you'll run up against a lot of language and requirements that don't seem to jibe with your project's intent. Keep your permit officer on speed dial and be prepared to ask a lot of clarifying questions. Moreover, depending on the type and scale of the project, you might trigger the need to pull several other related permits (e.g., electrical, tents, structural, traffic management, trash and recycling management, event insurance, vending, porta-potties). If this occurs, plan to spend more time and money on paperwork.

For this reason and others, we recommend being as vague as possible in describing your project during the application process, designing project elements to come in just under the thresholds of restrictive or prohibitive costs, and finding loopholes to help you deliver the project on budget and within a reasonable timeline.

Sound exhausting? It is. And although we've found permit officers to be great partners, very few cities offer a user-friendly and informative interface to help would-be applicants fully understand all that's involved at the outset. Even fewer have an easy permitting process designed to enable Tactical Urbanism projects.

It doesn't have to be this way, which is why some cities, such as San Francisco and Los Angeles, are actively developing a streamlined permitting process and creating a more inviting public interface so that citizens can play a more active role in improving the city.

San Francisco's Urban Prototyping Festival is a good example. Rather than continue dealing with 100 individual project applications over the course of the year, the city partnered in 2012 with foundations, private companies, and others to support the first festival geared to hacking the city. Jake Levitas, formerly of the sponsoring Gray Area Foundation, wrote, "We've been seeing a parallel between DIY urbanism and the DIY civic hacking worlds, and we wanted to bring these two communities together to see what possibilities could come out of that."[8] The festival attracted more than ninety groups pitching their projects and is set to return in 2015. Moreover, the city used the festival as a way to test out their own lean permitting chops and have since developed Living Innovation Zones that encourage and make easier the creation of temporary, flexible spaces for community interaction.[9]

Sanctioned or not, your project is an opportunity demonstrate what's possible to friends, neighbors, and city leaders. Remind them of this fact and help them reconsider easier ways to enable projects like yours. Chances are, you're not the only one who wants to contribute to your city in this way.

FINDING MATERIALS

If you've zeroed in on an opportunity site, raised any needed funds, and decided when to proceed, you'll still need materials to make it all happen. For starters, we recommend using borrowed, found, and recycled materials wherever possible. This is obviously the cheapest and most environmentally friendly option. It will also help you build relationships in your community and bring your donors into the project development process, which costs little more than transporting the materials and writing a thank-you note. However, in some cases you'll need to purchase materials to complete the project effectively. Many of these can be purchased at a discount if you know where and when to look.

We've found a few low-cost materials to be of great use. Straw waddles and orange traffic cones are great for changing the geometry of a street, and the new do-it-yourself traffic counter tool Waycount will help you keep track of its use.

However, it wouldn't be prudent to list every object or material we've ever used, so we've decided to instead to share some of our favorites and include a few tips about their use, procurement, and alternatives should you need them.

Paint

A little color will change the character of a place almost immediately. However, it can also get you in trouble when applied without permission, especially when used on the street. So unless you are carrying out a sanctioned intersection repair project or something similar, we recommend using temporary paint for all street surfaces. Crayola's Washable Sidewalk Paint is one option, and homemade paint is another (just mix a spoonful of powdered tempera paint, one half cup of water, and one-half cup of cornstarch). Each will have the desired short-term effect and will not take much work to remove at project's end. For buildings and vacant walls, the choice of paint will

LEFT: San Francisco's Urban Prototyping Festival. (Kay Cheng)

depend on the surface. And as long as you are not picky about color, already used "oops" paint is a bargain and may be found by the gallon at most paint and hardware stores. Finally, a cheaper and more temporary alternative is to simply use colored sidewalk chalk.

Landscaping

Trees, bushes, and plants change the character of an area almost instantly. The best place to find such greenery is a local nursery or big-box hardware store (such as Lowe's or Home Depot). Rather than buy dozens of plants and trees for a single weekend, you could explain the goals of your project and ask the nursery to lend you what you need in exchange for promoting their business as a project sponsor (this works well for higher-visibility, sanctioned projects). In some instances, stores, especially corporate ones, will simply write off the materials as a donation and give the materials away. Some nurseries will deliver and pick up only if you pay them a fee, so it's best to ask up front. And if you can't swing the price, you might compare the cost of renting or the time needed to borrow a truck to help transport the goods. If sourcing real plants is a challenge, you can approach a local movie set design or production company for temporary props, such as fake trees and bushes. These can be almost good as the real thing, as long as the props are in stock. Finally, remember that if the plants are out for as little as 24 hours, you'll need to water them to make sure they remain in good condition.

Shipping Pallets

Shipping pallets can be used for an incredible array of project elements: chairs, benches, tables, planters, a stage, low-rise walls, parklets, stadium seating, the list ends at the depth of your creativity. However, if you are struggling for ideas, there are many online guides and Pinterest pages that will show you a range of possibilities. Or you can simply visit Instructables (www.instructables.com) for direction. Fortunately, pallets are as ubiquitous as their applications. However, we suggest narrowing your search to warehouses and big-box stores that sell nontoxic hard goods, which will increase your chance of finding clean and sturdy pallets. For some project elements, you'll want pallets of a uniform size, so bring your tape measure or be prepared to find multiple pallet sources to meet your needs. Finally, for safety

The addition of temporary landscaping during a 2013 Tactical Urbanism Salon helped test one of the East Market Street redesign alternatives in Louisville, KY. (Mike Lydon)

purposes you'll want to look for pallets with a "HT" stamp on the side, not "MB." The former means that the pallet was heat-treated (good), and the latter means it was chemically treated with methyl bromide (bad, especially if you want to plant edibles). All new pallets are now required to have this code emblazoned on the side, so don't forget to look.

Traffic Tape
Traffic tape is not the cheapest material (between $80 and $120 for a 6-inch by 90-foot roll), but it's professional grade, reflective, and nonslip. You can also buy it online at desired widths (e.g., 4, 6, or 12 inches). If your budget allows for it, we recommend its use for all street projects that alter existing or add new pavement markings (e.g., bike lanes, parking stalls, crosswalks), especially if your project is intended to last more than a few days. A cheaper and still more temporary alternative is to use white duct tape. You'll be surprised how real it looks!

The Commons in Christchurch, New Zealand is an evolving and temporary public space installation located on the site of the former Crowne Plaza Hotel, which was demolished after the 2011 earthquake. (Clayton Prest)

Whatever you do, and whether sanctioned or not, remember to keep a list of materials used and the pricing for each element. This will help you stay organized and tally the cost so that you can communicate just how little you spent to make the changes. You can then send your list to others, with any needed adjustments, so that your project can be replicated, if and when it's a success.

Depending on the degree of permanence you are seeking, temporary materials should be capable of leaving no trace when they are ultimately removed. Matt Tomasulo's Walk Raleigh project (chapter 4) very consciously affixed signage to existing lamp posts using zip ties, which could be snipped with scissors and removed easily when the time came. Candy Chang ultimately used nonresidue stickers for her "I Wish This Was..." project in New Orleans. Borrowed plants can be returned to the nursery or given away to project participants. You get the idea.

Kent State Urban Design Collaborative Students apply traffic tape as part of the Pop-Up Rockwell project. (Kent State Urban Design Collaborative)

5. TEST: PUTTING THE BUILD–MEASURE–LEARN PROCESS TO GOOD USE

Now that you've selected a site, established what you'll be doing, and gathered the materials, it's time to test the project. At this point, failure is a real option, or at least some things may not go as planned, and that's okay—in fact that's the point!

The process used to test projects is like a streamlined version of the scientific method, or, as described in *The Lean Startup*, "build–measure–learn." That is to say, build the project prototype, measure its impact (over days, weeks, months, even years), and learn from the results. The three-step process may be repeated as often as needed until project proponents decide to either try something else entirely or become comfortable enough to invest for the long term. A concrete example of this process that played out on the global stage is the 5 years of tinkering and measuring in Times Square that has resulted in permanent infrastructure (see chapter 4). In many ways, this process is analogous to the urban design charrette process,

BUILD, MEASURE, LEARN

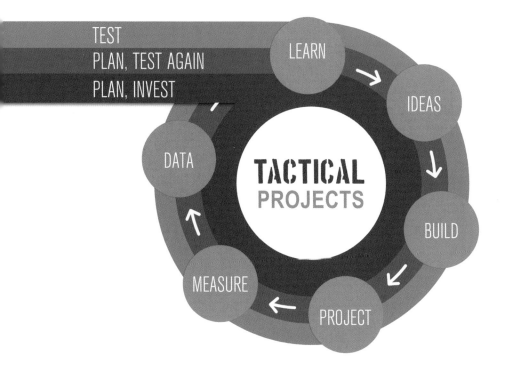

Build–measure–learn process. (The Street Plan Collaborative)

where ideas are solicited and vetted through the drafting and redrafting of plans in fast succession, only the feedback loops result in physical interventions, not paper plans.

BUILD

The "build" aspect of Tactical Urbanism takes the benefits of public input and the momentum of a design charrette and moves some part of the plan to early implementation. This short-term action can create a ripple effect of awareness, demand, and the realization that change is possible.

Participants at the Tactical Urbanism Salon in Boston try their hand at building pallet chairs. (The Street Plan Collaborative)

Thus, the act of building the project prototype has two fundamental values: One is the process—the collective act of *doing*—and the other is the tangible result of these efforts. The former provides a wonderful opportunity to build relationships in the community, add capacity for future projects, and create more champions for the project. The latter puts the built result on full display for all to observe, use, research, and critique. For sanctioned projects, the completion of the project prototype gives cities and the politicians that lead them a wonderful opportunity to communicate progress on already adopted plans, policies, and initiatives.

Of course, not every project will turn out as planned. So expect and plan for the unknown and be open to learning from the mistakes—there will be some!

MEASURE SUCCESS (AND LEARN FROM FAILURE)

Michael Bloomberg, the former mayor of New York City, famously said, "In God we trust. Everyone else bring data."[10] The statement, steeped in pragmatism, sums up his administration's approach to policy and decision making that helped make New York more livable. It also indicates the direction in which governments are heading. Big Data, open data, all data have become a flashpoint for those endeavoring to make well-informed and transparent decisions about the dynamics of city building. Just ask supporters of New York City's ongoing street transformation, who found a lot to like in a Department of Transportation that brought data, showing compelling before-and-after numbers validating the administration's break from the status quo approach to transportation and street design.

As important as measuring just about everything has become, Tactical Urbanism projects may be judged almost instantly, often upon delivery: a vacant lot is cleaned up and transformed into a pocket park where people gather, a single-car parking space is turned into bike parking, citizens hang replica speed limit signs directing motorists to drive slower, and it works—or maybe not. Ultimately, the value of Tactical Urbanism is derived from testing assumptions through physical design that can be viewed openly. But if you are not measuring the impact, you are writing only half the story.

Fortunately, measurement tools and key metrics against which to judge success are now more accessible to citizens and government officials than ever before. These include low-cost ways to count bicycle and pedestrian volumes, decibels, traffic speed, retail sales, and any number of other qualitative or quantitative data points that communicate success or failure.

The reason Tactical Urbanism works in the political sphere is that it helps unbundle the risk associated with altering the status quo. It helps us once again learn continuously what works and what doesn't, and that's the whole point.

LEARN

How cities learn has changed dramatically in recent years. Feedback loops have shortened, data have become more abundant, and it seems like we're fumbling a little less in the dark as our processes bring light to what works and what doesn't.

Perhaps no one demonstrates this new approach better than graduate students at Kent State's Urban Design Collaborative, who developed a week-long "complete and green street" experiment in 2012 along four blocks of Rockwell Avenue in downtown Cleveland.

RIGHT: Andrew Howard of Team Better Block records traffic speed. (Team Better Block)

Dubbed "Pop-Up Rockwell," the project was designed to push the envelope and serve as an interim step between the city's adoption of a new Complete and Green Streets Ordinance and permanent implementation. It included the city's first cycle track, bio-infiltration benches, improved transit waiting areas, and wind-animated public art.[11]

Thus, it was as much an exercise in building as it was in assessing the impact and learning—rapidly—what worked and what did not. Over the course of the week, students used time-lapse photography, film, interviews, and other forms of data collection. The project uncovered numerous lessons for future design efforts: Twice as many people cycled on the street as before, businesses were not ultimately bothered by the loss of parking, and buses could continue with their maneuvering. However, perhaps most important is that the group of students learned very quickly that their intersection design treatments (for the bikeway) could be further improved to prevent motorists from driving in the cycle track, that the public art could be made more clear, and that 1 week, though very valuable, is simply too short a time frame to get definitive results.

Rather than learn these lessons after years of planning and millions of dollars spent on permanent infrastructure, the students were able to build the project, measure the impact, and learn quickly what should be made part of the next project phase. From start to finish, this process took one semester, not years, and provided a smarter, more nimble, and more effective way to deliver on the promises of the city's recent planning initiatives so that money is not wasted with otherwise uninformed processes. If only most street design projects were developed this way!

Indeed, if some aspects of a project work well, then it's a good idea to double down on the positive outcomes while also learning from the elements that don't work so well. This "test and then invest" mentality is at the core of so many fields and should become the standard protocol for many kinds of urban planning and design projects.

Guiding Questions

The five-step design thinking process is simple in concept but full of nuanced considerations, which we hope we've helped you understand. However, for brevity's sake, we've put together the following cheat sheet. It includes a series of important guiding questions worth asking yourself and others before

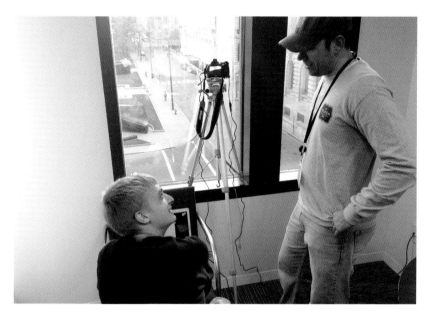

Documenting the effects of Pop-Up Rockwell. (Kent State Urban Design Collaborative)

undertaking a Tactical Urbanism project. This summary "code of ethics" maintains the structure of the five-step design thinking approach to Tactical Urbanism and was developed with Mariko Davidson, an urban planner who wrote her master's thesis on Tactical Urbanism at Harvard's Graduate School of Design. It's obviously calibrated for the development of Tactical Urbanism projects, but we believe most of the questions included can and should be applied to projects of all types.

Empathize

Understand for whom you are really planning or designing.

- Who is this project for?
- How many people have you talked to in the community?
- Do you need to become more familiar with the community?
- Who in the community will benefit? Who will not?
- Can you get more buy-in from your neighbors or the people who live and work near the project?
- How can your project proposal be broadened to further engage and support young, old, disabled, poor, disadvantaged, minority groups?

- Are there special needs in the community?
- Can the project be adjusted to reach a wider swath of users?
- Have you put yourself in the shoes of the least advantaged?
- Have you engaged a variety of stakeholders to help you with the project?

Define

Identify a specific opportunity site and clearly articulate the root causes of the problems that need to be addressed.

- What are the needs of the community?
- Can you shrink the scale of the site and scope of the project, at least temporarily?
- Does the problem exist elsewhere locally? Do the site conditions exist elsewhere?
- Is there any relevant history that might inform the future of the site?
- Have you used the Five Whys exercise to help define the root causes of the problem you seek to address?

Ideate

Research and develop ways to address the defined problem.

- Will your project ideas be developed alone, with a small group, or with a large assembly of people?
- Will the project actually provide an advantage over the status quo for an identified group of people?
- Is the project compatible with its social and physical context, both in scale and in scope?
- Can the project be easily understood by most people?
- Can the project be tested easily?
- Can the project be easily replicated elsewhere?
- Is the path to implementation clear and relatively hurdle free?
- Will you undertake a sanctioned or unsanctioned project approach?
- Is the project going to be visible to many others?
- What can be learned from other projects implemented in other similar contexts?

Prototype

Plan a project response that may be carried out quickly and without great expense.

- Have you articulated the proposed project's long-term goal?
- How can you ensure the continuation of your project after implementation?
- Once implemented, what is the impact? Can you measure it quantitatively? Qualitatively?
- Does it address the area's sustainability, accessibility, equity, and health? If not, can it be reshaped to address these issues?
- Can you identify and safely exploit opportunity within a framework?
- Are there any safety risks with the project?
- Who in your community can help you?
- Can you create partnerships to strengthen buy-in?

Test

Use the build–measure–learn process to implement the project and gather feedback.

- Do you have a variety of stakeholders to help you with the project?
- Are you planning for the unknown?
- Have you developed actionable metrics to use during the test?
- How will you communicate what you learn? Your successes and failures?

06 CONCLUSION: GO OUT AND USE THIS BOOK!

—

The freedom to make and remake our cities and ourselves is, I want to argue, one of the most precious yet most neglected of our human rights.

—DAVID HARVEY

Distinguished Professor of Anthropology and Geography, Graduate Center, CUNY

Our firm has been involved in documenting and applying Tactical Urbanism practices globally for the past 4 years. Let's be honest: 4 years is not that long! However, we've learned a great deal by *doing*—first by writing the Tactical Urbanism guides, then by working alongside passionate citizens, innovative government leaders, smart developers, and forward-thinking advocacy organizations.

What we've learned is that Tactical Urbanism did not just materialize; it has always been part of how we build cities. Human settlements existed for thousands of years as vernacular responses to practical everyday needs, long before any centralized, top-down citymaking endeavor was established. And as the David Harvey quote implies, it is innate in people to want to shape the environment that surrounds them. Yet in today's highly regulated and bureaucratic world, allowing for a citizen-led development of the city and the ritual use of public space is often never considered.

Why?

These approaches must be prioritized. An increasing number of citizens want to *co-develop* neighborhood projects rather than have city leaders and consultants alone lead the way, and for that reason (and others) we've expended a fair amount of energy defining the Tactical Urbanism movement in this book. We've also relished the opportunity to dig further into its history and to share a few of our favorite examples. But more than anything, it has served as a point of reflection.

We don't see Tactical Urbanism as a single idea. It is both an adaptation and an extension of the timeless principles that have always made our cities worth inhabiting. Our position is that the ideas presented in this book provide a critical and too often missing step in the journey toward creating still more compact, walkable, equitable, and, we hope, convivial places to live together.

To that end, we want to see our streets and neighborhoods live up to their potential. We want to see vibrant downtowns, with historic buildings adapted and reused for modern uses, less expensive and quickly implemented transit projects, and public works and planning departments that are more responsive to the needs of those they serve. Governments are positioned to make it easy for good things to happen in cities by removing onerous and outdated regulations; from making it easier to add "granny flats" to reducing the paperwork involved in infrastructure projects, to providing an easy-to-use parklet program, regulations must be reduced and the project delivery system simplified. And for God's sake, get it all online!

These are all goals that can be achieved by incorporating the many ideas presented in this book. But to get "lighter, cheaper, quicker" results, we must not only rethink existing processes for municipal and developer-led projects but enable the passionate co-creators, advocacy groups, and others striving for urban livability today, not in 50 years.

The term *Tactical Urbanism* has come to describe this movement. But although it's truly caught on, we are the first to recognize that it's another example of planning jargon, and that puts distance between people and those who serve them (i.e., we the authors and many of you readers). That's not our goal. So if you find that the term is offputting or inaccessible to some populations of people you work with and for, consider using something else. "Action planning" and "planning by doing" are two common replacements. No matter what you call the work, we hope that after you finish reading this book you'll understand that what truly matters is the scope and intent of the projects and the integrity of the process.

Finally, the growth of the Tactical Urbanism movement has come at a fascinating if not daunting moment in time. As rapid urbanization contin-ues, one thing is clear: Human, economic, and natural resources will only become more strained as we continue to grapple with global climate change and the diminishing returns of globalism. We have to do more with less— *doing* being the operative word. We're inspired by this challenge in our own work and are happy to have shared with you a more in-depth look at how others have done this successfully, but not without failures and setbacks. Ultimately, we challenge you to take action where it might matter to you most: in front of your house, on your street, or in your neighborhood. After all, if we can't work collectively—fellow citizens, government leaders, or both—to make these places better, we'll certainly have a hard time doing so at any larger scale.

So we can't guarantee that your $2,000 project will catalyze $2 million of municipal or private investment (should that even be the point?) or that the paint you put on the ground will quickly turn into your city's next beautiful town square, but we can promise that these things will never happen unless *someone* takes action. If you take anything away from this book, we hope you've learned that person is *you*. So stop reading and get started. Today!

NOTES

—

Chapter 01

1. Nabeel Hamdi, *The Placemaker's Guide to Building Community*, Earthscan Tools for Community Planning (London: Routledge, 2010).

2. Ethan Kent, "Rose Kennedy Greenway 'A Design Disaster,'" Project for Public Spaces blog, April 30, 2010, http://www.pps.org/blog/rose-kennedy-greenway-a-design-disaster/.

3. Editorial, "How to Fix the Greenway," *The Boston Globe*, April 18, 2010, http://www.boston.com/bostonglobe/editorial_opinion/editorials/articles/2010/04/18/how_to_fix_the_greenway/.

4. Robert Campbell, "How to Save the Greenway? Make It a Neighborhood," *The Boston Globe*, April 25, 2010, http://www.boston.com/ae/theater_arts/articles/2010/04/25/how_to_save_the_rose_kennedy_greenway_from_emptiness_and_disconnection/?page=full.

5. http://en.wikipedia.org/wiki/The_Toyota_Way (accessed 7/21/14).

6. http://theleanstartup.com/principles (accessed 7/21/14).

7. William H. Whyte, *City: Rediscovering the Center* (New York: Doubleday, 1989).

8. Jessica Grose, "Please, Pinterest, Stop Telling Me How to Repurpose Mason Jars: DIY Culture, Homemaking, and the End of Expertise," August 4, 2013, http://www.newrepublic.com/article/114144/pinterest-effect-rise-diy-and-end-expertise.

9. SPUR, "DIY Urbanism: Testing the Grounds for Social Change," *The Urbanist* 476 (September 2010), http://www.spur.org/publications/article/2010-09-01/diy-urbanism (accessed 7/21/2014).

10. Celeste Pagano, "DIY Urbanism: Property and Process in Grassroots City Building," *Marquette Law Review* 97 (2014), 1.

11. Parkside Park-In, Buffalo, NY, November 6, 2013, http://www.youtube.com/watch?v=JVhiVA1iqVs (accessed 7/21/14).

12. Alia Wong, "Don't Walk: Hawaii Pedestrians, Especially Elderly, Die at High Rate," *Honolulu Civil Beat*, September 2, 2012, http://www.civilbeat.com/articles/2012/09/04/17004-dont-walk-hawaii-pedestrians-especially-elderly-die-at-high-rate/.

13. The simplicity and nearly instant impact of this intervention type is captured brilliantly on one of the group's videos, where the pallet chairs are dropped next to a woman sitting on the sidewalk outside a popular coffee shop in Brooklyn. Looking puzzled at first, she soon moved off the ground and into one of the chairs. The coffee shop got the message. Within a few weeks one could spot benches out front during business hours.

14. "Penrith's Pop-Up Park to Stay," *Penrith City Gazette*, May 22, 2014, http://www.penrithcitygazette.com.au/story/2296693/penriths-pop-up-park-to-stay/.

15. Cassandra O'Connor, "Council to Build Second Pop-Up Park," *The Western Weekender*, May 8, 2014, http://www.westernweekender.com.au/index.php/news/2232-council-to-build-second-popup-park.

16. Fast Company Staff, "Design Thinking … What Is That?," *Fast Company*, http://www.fastcompany.com/919258/design-thinking-what.

17. Nabeel Hamdi, *Small Change: About the Art of Practice and the Limits of Planning in Cities* (London: Routledge, 2013), xix.

Chapter 02

1. Lewis Mumford, *The City in History: Its Origins, Its Transformations, and Its Prospects* (New York: Mariner Books, 1968), 5.

2. "The first true street of which we have a record may be in Khirokitia, a hilltop settlement of the sixth millennium BC in southern Cyprus…. By explicitly defining and articulating an outdoor space for the common good, the people assume a double responsibility: the upkeep of this space and its preservation as public property. A public way, by definition, belongs to everybody. Steady repair and alteration of the main street during its protracted life show that the community was not innocent of

'civic' duty." Spiro K. Kostoff, *The City Shaped: Urban Patterns and Meanings through History* (Thames & Hudson, Limited, 1999), 48–49. See also http://whc.unesco.org/en/list/848.

3. http://www.khirokitia.org/en/neolithic-len.

4. "Such spontaneous councils expressed the human consensus, not so much ruling and making new decisions as giving some immediate application to accepted rules and to decisions made in an immemorial past." Mumford, *City in History,* 19.

5. Albert Z. Guttenberg, "The Woonerf: A Social Invention in Urban Structure," *ITE Journal*, October 1981, http://www.ite.org/traffic/documents/JJA81A17.pdf.

6. Reid H. Ewing, "A Brief History of Traffic Calming," in *Traffic Calming: State of the Practice* (Washington, DC: ITE/FHWA, August 1999), http://www.ite.org/traffic/tcsop/chapter2.pdf.

7. Kostoff, *The City Shaped*, 43.

8. Frank Miranda, "Castra et Coloniae: The Role of the Roman Army in the Romanization and Urbanization of Spain," *Quaestio: The UCLA Undergraduate History Journal* (2002). Phi Alpha Theta: History Honors Society, UCLA Theta Upsilon Chapter, UCLA Department of History.

9. "The colonist had little time to get the lay of the land or explore the resources of a site: by simplifying his spatial order, he provided for a swift and roughly equal distribution of building lots." Mumford, *City in History*, 193.

10. Murray N. Rothbard, "Pennsylvania's Anarchist Experiment: 1681–1690," in *Conceived in Liberty*, Vol. 1, by Murray N. Rothbard (Auburn, AL: Ludwig von Mises Institute: Advancing Austrian Economics, Liberty, and Peace, July 8, 2005), http://mises.org/daily/1865.

11. Tuomi J. Forrest, "William Penn Plans the City," in *William Penn: Visionary Proprietor*, http://xroads.virginia.edu/~CAP/PENN/pnplan.html.

12. http://www.elfrethsalley.org.

13. "Canadian Aladdin houses were precut at the factory and shipped to the railway station closest to the customer. The lumber and materials were accompanied by a detailed set of blueprints and

construction manual. Aladdin boasted that anyone who could swing a hammer could build an Aladdin Home and they offered to pay $1 per knot for every knot you could find in a carload of Aladdin lumber. Imagine that guarantee today: The lumberyard would owe us money." Les Henry, "Mail-Order Houses," in *Before E-Commerce: A History of Canadian Mail-Order Catalogues*, Canadian Museum of History, http://www.civilization.ca/cmc/exhibitions/cpm/catalog/cat2104e.shtml.

14. "For the first time in the history of the world, middle class families in the late nineteenth century could reasonably expect to buy a detached home on an accessible lot....The real price of shelter in the United States was lower than in the Old World." Kenneth T. Jackson, *Crabgrass Frontier: The Suburbanization of the United States* (New York: Oxford University Press, 1985), 136.

15. "The houses in a streetcar suburb were generally narrow in width compared to later homes, and Arts and Crafts movement styles like the California Bungalow and American Foursquare were most popular. These houses were typically purchased by catalog and many of the materials arrived by railcar, with some local touches added as the house was assembled. The earliest streetcar suburbs sometimes had more ornate styles, including late Victorian and Stick. The houses of streetcar suburbs, whatever the style, tended to have prominent front porches, while driveways and built-in garages were rare, reflecting the pedestrian-focused nature of the streets when the houses were initially built. Setbacks between houses were not nearly as small as in older neighborhoods (where they were sometimes nonexistent), but houses were still typically built on lots no wider than 30 to 40 feet." Josef W. Konvitz, "Patterns in the Development of Urban Infrastructure," *American Urbanism: A Historiographical Overview* (Santa Barbara, CA: Greenwood Press, 1987), 204.

16. Alan Trachtenberg, *The Incorporation of America: Culture and Society in the Gilded Age* (New York: Macmillan, 2007), 231.

17. "World's Columbian Exposition," http://en.wikipedia.org/wiki/World's_Columbian_Exposition.

18. "The only harm of aged buildings to a city district or street is the

harm that eventually comes of nothing but old age—the harm that lies in everything being old and everything becoming worn out." Jane Jacobs, *The Death and Life of Great American Cities* (New York: Vintage, 1992, Reissue), 189.

19. Donald Appleyard, *Livable Streets* (Berkeley: University of California Press, 1982); Carmen Hass-Klau, *The Pedestrian and City Traffic* (New York: Wiley, 1990); "Play Streets," Center for Active Design, http://centerforactivedesign.org/playstreets/. "Reclaiming the Residential Street as Play Space," *International Play Journal* 4 (1996): 91–97, http://ecoplan.org/children/general/tranter.htm; "Pedestrians," *New York City DOT*, http://www.nyc.gov/html/dot/html/pedestrians/publicplaza-sites.shtml; "PAL Play Streets," Police Athletic League, http://www.palnyc.org/800-PAL-4KIDS/Program.aspx?id=30; "History," Police Athletic League, http://www.palnyc.org/800-pal-4kids/history.aspx; "Play Streets," *Missouri Revised Statutes: Chapter 300, Model Traffic Ordinance*, http://www.moga.mo.gov/statuteSearch/StatHtml/3000000348.htm; "About Play Streets," *Partnership for a Healthier America*, http://ahealthieramerica.org/play-streets/about-play-streets/; "Plan Safe Streets for Children's Play," *New York Times*, May 7, 1909, http://query.nytimes.com/mem/archive-free/pdf?res=9F01E7DF1E31E733A25754C0A9639C946897D6CF; http://www.londonplay.org.uk/file/1333.pdf.

20. Claire Duffin, "Streets Are Alive with the Sound of Children Playing," *Telegraph*, February 22, 2014, http://www.telegraph.co.uk/health/children_shealth/10654330/Streets-are-alive-with-the-sound-of-children-playing.html.

21. Ibid.

22. Bonnie Ora Sherk interview, August 2013.

23. Peter Cavagnaro, "Q & A: Bonnie Ora Sherk and the Performance of Being," University of California, Berkeley Art Museum & Pacific Film Archive, June 2012, http://blook.bampfa.berkeley.edu/2012/06/q-a-bonnie-ora-sherk-and-the-performance-of-being.html.

24. "Early Public Landscape Art by Bonnie Ora Sherk Featured in SFMOMA Show—SF's Original "Parklet," *A Living Library*, December 2011, http://www.alivinglibrary.org/blog/art-landscape

-architecture-systemic-design/early-art-bonnie-ora-sherk-featured
-sfmoma-show.

25. "The Perambulating Library," Mealsgate.org.uk—The George
Moore Connection, *The British Workman*, February 1, 1857, http://
www.mealsgate.org.uk/perambulating-library.php.

26. From *On the Trail of the Book Wagon*, by Mary Titcomb, two papers
read at the meeting of the American Library Association, June 1909.

27. Ward Andrews, "The Mobile Library: The Sketchbook Project
Gets a Totable Home + Tour," Design.org, http://design.org/blog/
mobile-library-sketchbook-project-gets-totable-home-tour.

28. Todd Feathers, "Mobile City Hall Truck to Rotate through Boston
Neighborhoods," *The Boston Globe*, June 15, 2013, http://www
.bostonglobe.com/metro/2013/06/25/mobile-city-hall-truck-rotate
-through-boston-neighborhoods/Uyf66jFaC1q0pi03ff6H6M/story
.html.

29. Liz Danzico, "Histories of the Traveling Libraries," *Bobulate: for
Intentional Organization*, October 26, 2011, http://bobulate.com/
post/11938328379/histories-of-the-traveling-libraries; Orty Ortwein,
"Before the Automobile: The First Mobile Libraries," *Bookmobiles:
A History*, May 3, 2013, http://bookmobiles.wordpress.
com/2013/05/03/before-the-automobile-the-first-mobile-libraries/;
"Mobile Libraries," American Library Association, http://www.ala
.org/tools/mobile-libraries; Leo Hickman, "Is the Mobile Library
Dead?" *The Guardian*, April 7, 2010, http://www.theguardian.com/
books/2010/apr/07/mobile-libraries.

30. "Bouquinistes of Paris," *French Moments*, http://www.french
moments.eu/bouquinistes-of-paris/.

31. Kristin Kusnic Michel, "Paris' Riverside Bouquinistes," *Rick Steves'
Europe*, http://www.ricksteves.com/watch-read-listen/read/articles/
paris-riverside-bouquinistes.

32. Olivia Snaije, "Paris' Seine-Side Bookselling *Bouquinistes* Tout
Trinkets, but City Hall Cries 'Non,'" *Publishing Perspectives*,
October 19, 2010, http://publishingperspectives.com/2010/10/
paris-seine-side-bookselling-bouquinistes/Michel; "Paris' Riverside
Bouquinistes," http://www.ricksteves.com/plan/destinations/
france/bouquinistes.htm.

33. "Rhode Island (RI) Diners," VisitNewEngland.com, http://www
    .visitri.com/rhodeisland_diners.html.

34. This is still in service today as the last known horse-drawn lunch
    wagon.

35. Kristine Hass, "Hoo Am I? A Look at the Owl Night Lunch
    Wagon," *The Henry Ford*, May 15, 2012, http://blog.thehenryford
    .org/2012/05/hoo-am-i-a-look-at-the-owl-night-lunch-wagon/.

36. Gustavo Arellano, "Tamales, L.A.'s Original Street Food," *Los
    Angeles Times*, September 8, 2011, http://articles.latimes.com/2011/
    sep/08/food/la-fo-tamales-20110908.

37. Jesus Sanchez, "King Taco Got Start in Old Ice Cream Van," *Los
    Angeles Times*, November 16, 1987, http://articles.latimes.com/1987
    -11-16/business/fi-14263_1_ice-cream-truck; Romy Oltuski,
    "The Food Truck: A Photographic Retrospective," *FlavorWire*,
    September 27, 2011, http://flavorwire.com/213637/the-food-truck
    -a-photographic-retrospective/view-all/; "Food Truck," Wikipedia,
    http://en.wikipedia.org/wiki/Food_truck; Anna Brones, "Food
    History: The History of Food Trucks," *Ecosalon*, June 20, 2013,
    http://ecosalon.com/food-history-of-food-trucks/; Richard
    Myrick, "The Complete History of American Food Trucks,"
    Mobile Cuisine, July 2, 2012, http://mobile-cuisine.com/business/
    the-history-of-american-food-trucks/3/.

38. Stephanie Buck and Lindsey McCormack, "The Rise of the Social
    Food Truck [INFOGRAPHIC]," *Mashable*, August 4, 2011, http://
    mashable.com/2011/08/04/food-truck-history-infographic/.

39. *A 1977 Mexican food vendor busted by the police for violating new
    ordinances controlling the sale of street food*, 1977, http://flavorwire
    .files.wordpress.com/2011/09/john-griffith-taco-cart-busted-dec
    -1977-can8600f-600x5001.jpg?w=598&h=463.

40. Don Babwin, "Chicago Food Trucks: City Council Overwhelmingly
    Approves Mayor's Ordinance," *Huffington Post,* July 25, 2012,
    http://www.huffingtonpost.com/2012/07/25/chicago-food-trucks
    -alder_0_n_1701249.html.

41. Bill Thompson, "The Chuck Wagon," American Chuck Wagon
    Association, http://americanchuckwagon.org/chuck-wagon-history
    .html.

42. "Nevertheless, we recognize indefinable sense of well-being and which we want to return to, time and again. So that original notion of ritual, of repeated celebration or reverence, is still inherent in the phrase. It is not a temporary response, for it persists and brings us back, reminding us of previous visits." John Brinckerhoff Jackson, *A Sense of Place, a Sense of Time* (New Haven, CT: Yale University Press, 1994).

Chapter 03

1. "Urban Population Growth," *World Health Organization*, http:// www.who.int/gho/urban_health/situation_trends/urban_ population_growth_text/en/; Neal R. Peirce, Curtis W. Johnson, and Farley M. Peters, "Century of the City: No Time to Lose," The Rockefeller Foundation, http://www.rockefellerfoundation .org/blog/century-city-no-time-lose.

2. Derek Thompson and Jordan Weissman, "The Cheapest Generation," August 22, 2012, http://www.theatlantic.com/ magazine/archive/2012/09/the-cheapest-generation/309060/.

3. Brandon Schoettle and Michael Sivak, "The Reasons for the Recent Decline in Young Driver Licensing in the U.S.," University of Michigan Transportation Research Institute, August 2013, http:// deepblue.lib.umich.edu/bitstream/handle/2027.42/99124/102951.pdf.

4. Robert Steuteville, "Millennials, Even Those with Children, Are Multimodal and Urban," *Better Cities and Towns*, October 2, 2013, http://bettercities.net/article/millennials-even-those-children-are -multimodal-and-urban-20713.

5. Nate Berg, "America's Growing Urban Footprint," *City Lab*, March 28, 2012, http://www.theatlanticcities.com/neighborhoods/ 2012/03/americas-growing-urban-footprint/1615/.

6. Herbert Munschamp, "Architecture View: Can New Urbanism Find Room for the Old?" *The New York Times*, June 2, 1996, http:// www.nytimes.com/1996/06/02/arts/architecture-view-can-new -urbanism-find-room-for-the-old.html?pagewanted=all&src=pm.

7. Jordan Weissman, "America's Lost Decade Turns 12: Even the Rich Are Worse Off Than Before," *The Atlantic*, September 17,

2013, http://www.theatlantic.com/business/archive/2013/09/
americas-lost-decade-turns-12-even-the-rich-are-worse-off-than
-before/279744/.

8. Tony Schwartz, "Relax! You'll Be More Productive," *The New York Times*, February 9, 2013, http://www.nytimes.com/2013/02/10/opinion/sunday/relax-youll-be-more-productive.html?pagewanted=all&_r=0.

9. Jed Kolko, "Home Prices Rising Faster in Cities Than in the Suburbs—Most of All in Gayborhoods," *Trulia Trends: Real Estate Data for the Rest of Us*, June 25, 2013, http://trends.truliablog.com/2013/06/home-prices-rising-faster-in-cities/.

10. Leigh Gallagher, *The End of the Suburbs: Where the American Dream Is Moving* (New York: Penguin, 2013), 188.

11. Conor Dougherty and Robbie Whelan, "Cities Outpace Suburbs in Growth," *The Wall Street Journal*, June 28, 2012, http://online.wsj.com/news/articles/SB10001424052702304830704577493032619987956.

12. "Suburban Poverty in the News," *Confronting Poverty in America*, http://confrontingsuburbanpoverty.org/blog/.

13. Emily Badger, "The Suburbanization of Poverty," *City Lab,* May 20, 2013, http://www.theatlanticcities.com/jobs-and-economy/2013/05/suburbanization-poverty/5633/.

14. Center for Neighborhood Technology, "Losing Ground: The Struggle of Moderate-Income Households to Afford the Rising Costs of Housing and Transportation," October 2012, http://www.nhc.org/media/files/LosingGround_10_2012.pdf.

15. Joshua Franzel, "The Great Recession, U.S. Local Governments, and e-Government Solutions," *PM Magazine* 92, no. 8 (2010), http://webapps.icma.org/pm/9208/public/pmplus1.cfm?author=Joshua%20Franzel&title=The%20Great%20Recession%2C%20U.S.%20Local%20Governments%2C%20and%20e-Government%20Solutions.

16. "Government Spending in the US," http://www.usgovernmentspending.com/local_spending_2010USrn.

17. Karen Thoreson and James H. Svara, "Award-Winning Local Government Innovations, 2008," *The Municipal Year Book 2009* (Washington, DC: ICMA).

18. Richard Stallman, "On Hacking," Richard Stallman's personal site, http://stallman.org/articles/on-hacking.html.

19. Brian Davis, "On Broadway, Tactical Urbanism," *faslanyc: Speculative Histories, Landscapes and Instruments, and Latin American Landscape Architecture*, June 6, 2010, http://faslanyc.blogspot.com/search/label/ tactical%20urbanism.

20. Emily Jarvis, "How Radical Connectivity Is Changing the Way Government Operates," *Govloop*, May 10, 2013, http://www.govloop .com/profiles/blogshow-radical-connectivity-is-changing-the-way -gov-operates-plus-yo.

21. "One of the top 12 trends for 2012 as named by the communications firm Euro RSCG Worldwide is that employees in the Gen Y, or millennial, demographic—those born between roughly 1982 and 1993—are overturning the traditional workday." Dan Schwabel, "The Beginning of the End of the 9–5 Workday?" *Time*, December 21, 2011, http://business.time.com/2011/12/21/the-beginning-of-the -end-of-the-9-to-5-workday/#ixzz2lmQ6xJSM.

22. Authors William Strauss and Neil Howe wrote about the Millennials in *Generations: The History of America's Future, 1584 to 2069* and consider Millennials as being born between 1982 and 2004. The Pew Research Center places these dates at 1981–2000. Either way, these figures show that 48,977,000 workers are on the employment sheets, although the numbers may be skewed depending on how nontraditional work schedules fit into the data. Either way, employment as measured in the civilian labor force will not grow much over the next decade, meaning the Millennials will represent a larger piece of the employment pie. "Labor Force Statistics from the Current Population Survey," Bureau of Labor Statistics, February 12, 2014, http://www.bls.gov/cps/cpsaat03.htm.

23. Richard Florida, *The Rise of the Creative Class: And How It's Transforming Work, Leisure, Community and Everyday Life* (New York: Basic Books, 2002), 166.

24. "Raymond on Open Source," *New Learning: Transformational Designs for Pedagogy and Assessment*, http://newlearningonline.com/ literacies/chapter-1/raymond-on-open-source.

25. Ibid.

26. Jeremy Rifkin, "The Rise of Anti-Capitalism," *The New York Times*, March 15, 2014, http://www.nytimes.com/2014/03/16/opinion/sunday/the-rise-of-anti-capitalism.html?_r=0.

27. Joshua Franzel, "The Great Recession, U.S. Local Governments, and e-Government Solutions," http://webapps.icma.org/pm/9208/public/pmplus1.cfm?author=Joshua%20Franzel&title=The%20Great%20Recession%2C%20U.S.%20Local%20Governments%2C%20and%20e-Government%20Solutions.

28. "The workforce becomes increasingly urban, continuing a long trend, agriculture, which has under 4 million jobs or less than 3 percent of all employment, is projected to decline by 24,000 more jobs over the period 1996 to 2006." "4—Workplace," US Department of Labor, http://www.dol.gov/oasam/programs/history/herman/reports/futurework/report/chapter4/main.htm.

29. "Millennials in Adulthood: Detached from Institutions, Networked with Friends," *Pew Research: Social & Demographic Trends*, March 7, 2014, http://www.pewsocialtrends.org/2014/03/07/millennials-in-adulthood/.

30. http://www.citylab.com/tech/2013/12/rise-civic-tech/7765/.

31. Ioby, "Ioby Brings Neighborhood Projects to Life, Block by Block," http://www.ioby.org/.

32. Volodymyr V. Lysenko and Kevin C. Desouza, "Role of Internet-Based Information Flows and Technologies in Electoral Revolutions: The Case of Ukraine's Orange Revolution," *First Monday* 15, no. 9-6 (2010), http://firstmonday.org/ojs/index.php/fm/article/view/2992/2599.

33. Pew Research Center, National Election Studies, Gallup, ABC/Washington Post, CBS/New York Times, and CNN polls. From 1976 to 2010 the trend line represents a three-survey moving average. http://www.people-press.org/2013/10/18/trust-in-government-interactive/.

34. Theda Skocpol and Morris P. Fiorina, eds., *Civic Engagement in American Democracy* (Washington, DC: Brookings Institution Press, 2004).

35. Second Regional Plan, Stanley B. Tankel, Boris Bushkarev, and William B. Shore, eds., *Urban Design Manhattan: Regional Plan*

Association (New York: The Viking Press, 1969), http://library.rpa
.org/pdf/RPA-Plan2-Urban-Design-Manhattan.pdf.

36. Marc Santora, "City Gives the Garden's Owners a Deadline on
Penn Station," *The New York Times*, May 23, 2013, http://www.
nytimes.com/2013/05/24/nyregion/madison-square-garden-told-to
-fix-penn-station-or-move-out.html.

37. Ada Louise Huxtable, "Farewell to Penn Station," *The New York
Times*, October 30, 1963 (accessed 7/13/2010). (The editorial goes
on to say that "we will probably be judged not by the monuments
we build but by those we have destroyed," http://query.nytimes
.com/gst/abstract.html?res=9407EFD8113DE63BBC4850DFB6
678388679EDE). The Landmarks Preservation Commission
was established in 1965 when Mayor Robert Wagner signed the
local law creating the commission and giving it its power. The
Landmarks Law was enacted in response to New Yorkers' growing
concern that important physical elements of the city's history were
being lost despite the fact that these buildings could be reused.
Events such as the demolition of the architecturally distinguished
Pennsylvania Station in 1963 increased public awareness of the
need to protect the city's architectural, historical, and cultural
heritage. http://www.nyc.gov/html/lpc/html/about/about.shtml.

38. Robert Moses once held 12 positions of power in New York City
and New York State. For the biography, see Robert Caro's *The
Power Broker: Robert Moses and the Fall of New York* (New York:
Vintage Books, 1975).

39. Paul Davidoff, "Advocacy and Pluralism in Planning," *Journal of
the American Institute of Planners* 31, no. 4 (1965): 331–338, https://
www.planning.org/pas/memo/2007/mar/pdf/JAPA31No4.pdf.

40. Adam Bednar, "Hampden's DIY Crosswalks," *North Baltimore
Patch*, September 10, 2013, http://northbaltimore.patch.com/
articles/hampden-s-diy-crosswalks.

Chapter 04

1. Peter Kageyama, *For the Love of Cities* (St. Petersburg, FL:
Creative Cities Productions, 2011), 9.

2. Ibid., 7–8.

3. Jan C. Semenza, "The Intersection of Urban Planning, Art, and Public Health: The Sunnyside Piazza," *American Public Health Association* 93, no. 9 (2003): 1439–1441, http://www.ncbi.nlm.nih.gov/pmc/articles/PMC1447989/.

4. Lakeman interview, January 21, 2014, by Mike Lydon.

5. Ibid.

6. Jhon, interview with Mark Lakeman, *Many Mouths One Stomach*, http://www.manymouths.org/2009/08/turning-space-into-place-portlands-city-repair-project/.

7. "Mark Lakeman," in *Social Environmental Architects: "Designing the Future" Art Exhibit*, http://socialenvironmentalarchitects.wordpress.com/mark-lakeman/ (accessed 12/30/2013).

8. Ibid.

9. Lakeman interview, January 21, 2014, by Mike Lydon.

10. http://www.planetizen.com/node/11994.

11. Stuart Cowan, Mark Lakeman, Jenny Leis, Daniel Lerch, and Jan C. Semenza, *The City Repair Project*, http://www.inthefield.info/city_repair.pdf (accessed 12/31/2013).

12. Ibid.

13. http://daily.sightline.org/2011/11/28/coloring-inside-the-lanes/.

14. http://www.inthefield.info/city_repair.pdf (accessed 12/31/2013).

15. Lerch interview, December 19, 2013, by Mike Lydon.

16. Alyse Nelson, "Coloring Inside the Lanes," *Sightline Daily: News & Views for a Sustainable Northwest*, November 28, 2011, http://daily.sightline.org/2011/11/28/coloring-inside-the-lanes/ (accessed 1/1/2014).

17. Cornelius Swart, "Village Building Convergence Creates Murals, Relationships in North Portland," *Oregon Live*, May 31, 2012, http://www.oregonlive.com/portland/index.ssf/2012/05/village_building_convergence_c.html.

18. Alyse Nelson and Tim Shuck, "City Repair Project Case Study," http://courses.washington.edu/activism/cityrepair.htm (accessed 12/31/2013).

19. "Activities and Results," Depave, http://depave.org/about/results/ (accessed 1/1/2013).

20. Jan C. Semenza, "The Intersection of Urban Planning, Art, and

Public Health: The Sunnyside Piazza," *American Journal of Public Health* 93 (2003): 1439–1441, http://www.ncbi.nlm.nih.gov/pmc/articles/PMC1447989/ (accessed 1/1/2014).

21. Sandra A. Ham, Caroline A. Macera, and Corina Lindley, "Trends in Walking for Transportation in the United States, 1995 and 2001," *Preventing Chronic Disease* 4, no. 2 (2005), http://www.ncbi.nlm.nih.gov/pmc/articles/PMC1435711/.

22. Jeff Speck, *Walkable City: How Downtown Can Save America, One Step at a Time* (New York: North Point Press, 2012), 4.

23. Patrick C. Doherty and Christopher B. Leinberger, "The Next Real Estate Boom," *Brookings*, November 2010, http://www.brookings.edu/research/articles/2010/11/real-estate-leinberger.

24. Tomasulo interview, February 12, 2014, by Mike Lydon. All quotes from Tomasulo in this chapter are from this interview.

25. Ibid.

26. Emily Badger, "Guerrilla Wayfinding in Raleigh," *City Lab*, February 6, 2012, http://www.citylab.com/tech/2012/02/guerilla-wayfinding-raleigh/1139/.

27. Emily Badger, "Raleigh's Guerrilla Wayfinding Signs Deemed Illegal," *City Lab*, February 27, 2012, http://www.citylab.com/tech/2012/02/raleighs-guerrilla-wayfinding-signs-deemed-illegal/1341/.

28. Larchlion, "The Deep Ellum Better Block," Walkable DFW: Restoring a City to Walkability, November 1, 2010, http://www.carfreeinbigd.com/2010/11/deep-ellum-better-block.html.

29. Jason Roberts interview, August 7, 2013, by Mike Lydon.

30. Jason Roberts, "The Better Block Project," Bike Friendly Oak Cliff blog, March 26, 2010, http://bikefriendlyoc.org/2010/03/26/the-better-block-project/.

31. Robert Wilonsky, "Jason Roberts and the Better Block'ers Dare You to Build a Better Ross Avenue in Three Days," *Dallas Observer* blogs, May 4, 2011, http://blogs.dallasobserver.com/unfairpark/2011/05/jason_roberts_and_the_better_b.php.

32. Jason Roberts interview, August 7, 2013, by Mike Lydon.

33. Ibid.

34. "Living Plaza," http://www.dallascityhall.com/citydesign_studio/LivingPlaza.html.

35. Lisa Gray, "Gray: Building a Better Block," *Houston Chronicle*, June 28, 2010, http://www.chron.com/entertainment/article/Gray-Building-a-better-block-1711370.php.

36. "TEDxOU: Jason Roberts: How to Build a Better Block," delivered January 2012, Norman, Oklahoma, uploaded February 21, 2012, https://www.youtube.com/watch?v=ntwqVDzdqAU.

37. Angie Schmitt, "Q&A with Jason Roberts, the Brains Behind 'Better Blocks,'" Streetsblog USA, May 31, 2013, http://usa.streetsblog.org/2013/05/31/qa-with-jason-roberts-the-visionary-behind-the-better-block/.

38. "Better Block Drive Started," *Atlanta Daily World*, May 9, 1942; ProQuest Historical Newspapers: *Atlanta Daily World* (1931–2003).

39. "Operation Better Block Opens Day Care Center," *New York Amsterdam News*, December 12, 1970, http://ezproxy.lib.indiana.edu/login?url=http://search.proquest.com/docview/226650847?accountid=11620.

40. "Upland in 'Operation Better Block' Drive," *New Pittsburgh Courier* (1966–1981), City Edition, March 20, 1971, p. 6.

41. The Trust for Public Land, "The Economic Benefits and Fiscal Impact of Parks and Open Space in Nassau and Suffolk Counties, New York," 2010, http://cloud.tpl.org/pubs/ccpe--nassau-county-park-benefits.pdf.

42. "Parks for People: Miami," The Trust for Public Land, https://www.tpl.org/our-work/parks-for-people/parks-people-miami.

43. "Transportation Cost and Benefit Analysis II: Parking Costs," Victoria Transport Policy Institute, http://www.vtpi.org/tca/tca0504.pdf.

44. UCLA Toolkit, "Reclaiming the Right-of-Way: A Toolkit for Creating and Implementing Parklets," *UCLA Complete Streets Initiative*, September 2012, Luskin School of Public Affairs.

45. Pavement to Parks, "San Francisco Parklet Manual," San Francisco Planning Department, February 2013, http://sfpavementtoparks.sfplanning.org/docs/SF_P2P_Parklet_Manual_1.0_FULL.pdf.

46. "Parking Meter Party!" tlchamilton blog, July 9, 2001, http://tlchamilton.wordpress.com/2001/07/09/parking-meter-party/.

47. "Portfolio: Park(ing)," Rebar, November 16, 2005, http://rebar

group.org/parking/.

48. "About Park(ing) Day," Park(ing) Day, Rebar Group, http://park ingday.org/about-parking-day/.

49. Blaine Merker, 2013.

50. "Portfolio: Park(ing)," Rebar, http://rebargroup.org/parking/.

51. Lisa Taddeo, "Janette Sadik-Khan: Urban Reengineer," *Esquire*, http://www.esquire.com/features/brightest-2010/janette-sadik -khan-1210.

52. "New York City Streets Renaissance," Project for Public Spaces, http://www.pps.org/projects/new-york-city-streets-renaissance/.

53. Ibid.

54. Jennifer 8. Lee, "Sturdier Furniture Replaces Times Square Lawn Chairs," *The New York Times* blog, August 17, 2009, http://city room.blogs.nytimes.com/2009/08/17/sturdier-furniture-replaces -times-square-lawn-chairs/?_php=true&_type=blogs&_r=0.

55. All pilot project results sourced from "Pedestrians: Broadway," New York City DOT, http://www.nyc.gov/html/dot/html/ pedestrians/broadway.shtml.

56. "Mayor Bloomberg, Transportation Commissioner Sadik-Khan and Design and Construction Commissioner Burney Cut Ribbon on First Phase of Permanent Times Square Reconstruction," *Official Website of the City of New York*, December 23, 2013, http:// www1.nyc.gov/office-of-the-mayor/news/432-13/mayor-bloomberg -transportation-commissioner-sadik-khan-design-construction -commissioner/#/0.

57. Ibid.

58. Roberto Brambilla and Gianna Longo, *For Pedestrians Only: Planning, Design, and Management of Traffic-Free Zones* (New York: Whitney Library of Design, 1977), 8.

59. Dorina Pojani, "American Downtown Pedestrian "Malls": Rise, Fall, and Rebirth," *Territorio* 173–190, http://www.academia .edu/2098773/American_downtown_pedestrian_malls_rise_fall _and_rebirth.

60. "Privately Owned Public Space," New York City Planning: Department of City Planning, City of New York, http://www.nyc .gov/html/dcp/html/pops/pops.shtml.

61. William Whyte, *The Social Life of Small Urban Spaces* (New York: Project for Public Spaces, Inc, 2001), http://www.nyc.gov/html/dcp/html/pops/pops.shtml.

62. All Wade quotes and information sourced from an interview in the spring of 2014.

63. New York City DOT, "Measuring the Street: New Metrics for 21st Century Streets," http://www.nyc.gov/html/dot/downloads/pdf/2012-10-measuring-the-street.pdf.

64. Stephen Miller, "Ped Plazas in Low-Income Neighborhoods Get $800,000 Boost from Chase," Streets Blog NYC, November 26, 2013, http://www.streetsblog.org/2013/11/26/800000-from-chase -to-help-maintain-up-to-20-plazas-over-two-years/.

65. Pavement to Parks, San Francisco Planning Department, http://pavementtoparks.sfplanning.org/.

Chapter 05

1. "Design Thinking," Wikipedia, http://en.wikipedia.org/wiki/Design_thinking.

2. Eric Ries, *The Lean Startup: How Constant Innovation Creates Radically Successful Businesses* (New York: Crown Publishing Group, 2011).

3. Josh Zelman, "(Founder Stories) Eric Ries: On 'Vanity Metrics' and 'Success Theater,'" *Tech Crunch*, September 24, 2011, http://techcrunch.com/2011/09/24/founder-stories-eric-ries-vanity-metrics/.

4. Everett M. Rogers, *Diffusion of Innovations* (New York: Free Press of Glencoe, 1962).

5. Tony Burchyns, "Hero's Welcome for Vallejo's Crosswalk Painter," *Daily Democrat*, June 1, 2013, http://www.dailydemocrat.com/ci_23369425/heros-welcome-vallejos-crosswalk-painter?source =most_viewed.

6. Ibid.

7. "The Outlook for Debt and Equity Crowdfunding in 2014," *Venture Beat*, January 14, 2014, http://venturebeat.com/2014/01/14/the-outlook-for-debt-and-equity-crowdfunding-in-2014/.

8. Aaron Sankin, "Urban Prototyping Festival Redefines San Francisco's Public Space," *Huffington Post*, October 24, 2012, http://

www.huffingtonpost.com/2012/10/24/urban-prototyping-festival
_n_2007661.html.

9.   "Living Innovation Zones: Same Streets, Different Ideas," The
Mayor's Office of Civic Innovation and San Francisco Planning
Department, http://liz.innovatesf.com/.

10.   "Bye-Bye, Bloomberg: Pondering the Meaning of New York's
Billionaire Mayor," *The Economist*, November 2, 2013, http://www
.economist.com/news/united-states/21588855-pondering-meaning
-new-yorks-billionaire-mayor-bye-bye-bloomberg.

11.   "Pop Up Rockwell," Cleveland Urban Design Collaborative, Kent
State University, http://www.cudc.kent.edu/pop_up_city/rockwell/.